the World of the Cat

ESTHER J.J. VERHOEF-VERHALLEN

 **REBO** PRODUCTIONS

©1997 Rebo Productions b.v., The Netherlands
©1997 Published by Rebo Productions Ltd.
text: Esther Verhoef
cover design: Ton Wienbelt, The Netherlands
coordination and production: TextCase, The Netherlands
picture editing: Marieke Uiterwijk
editing: Ireen Niessen
typesetting: Hof&Land Typografie, The Netherlands
translation: Euro Business Translations, The Netherlands

ISBN 1 901094 65 0

Contents

Foreword

The enigma that is the cat has intrigued mankind for thousands of years. Cats were worshipped as gods in ancient Egypt, they were regarded as valuable gifts in the golden age of trade, and they were reviled and tortured in the Middle Ages. Nowadays, they have an important place as a much-loved pet. In the long history that mankind shares with the cat, it is mankind whose attitude to cats has constantly changed and adapted. Religion has been a major factor. The cat, however, has always remained itself. Unlike dogs and horses, cats never allow themselves to be subjected to the whims of their owners. They curl up on our laps in the evening and they condescend to let us share their lives, but they always retain their own identity. Although cats have been an important part of man's life since the dawn of human memory, it is only in the twentieth century that people have become interested in feline behaviour. All sorts of behaviours have been analyzed by dedicated researchers who have found explanations for many remarkable traits. It is in the last century, too, that the breeding of pedigree cats has really taken off.
Nowadays, alongside the innumerable domestic cats and moggies, there are close to seventy recognized and unrecognized breeds of cat throughout the world, in an amazingly varied range of coat colours. Many of these cats, noble and humble alike, are to be found in this book, together with information about wild cats, the turbulent history of the cat, and choosing and caring for a cat. I derived immense pleasure from writing this book and photographing the cats in all their guises. I hope you enjoy reading this book as much as I enjoyed producing it.

Esther J.J. Verhoef-Verhallen

Sumatran tiger

Wild cats

Wild cats occur virtually everywhere in the world. We find them on the vast, sweltering African plains, in the humid jungle swamps of Asia and on the snow-capped mountains of North America and Siberia.

Their physical build, adapted to the climate and habitat, their hunting methods and the length, thickness and colour of their coats have enabled the different species of the cat family to survive the harshest conditions.

Lion cubs

Right: Tigers conceal themselves in dense scrub and ambush their prey

Subfamilies

Broadly speaking, the cat family can be divided into three distinct subfamilies. The subfamily Pantherinae includes the big cats - lions, tigers, leopards, jaguars and lynxes. The subfamily Felinae contains the smaller wild cats, the most familiar among them being the serval, the African golden cat, the puma, the ocelot, the fishing cat, the black-footed cat and the wild cat.

The third group consists of a single species, the cheetah, which because of its specific characteristics cannot be put into either of the other two subfamilies.

Specific adaptations

The one thing all wild cats have in common is that they have to hunt to survive. Their build and musculature are designed for the purpose. Most wild cats, and many of the domesticated breeds too, have strongly muscled hind legs that are longer than the front legs. This gives them immense strength and propulsion for leaping. Some of the big cats can also climb extremely well - and will choose to sleep on a

Like their wild cousins, our domestic cats have retractable claws. This Cornish Rex kitten is showing his

Most members of the cat family only hunt when they are hungry

sturdy branch. Their physical characteristics enable them to move at top speed from total immobility in an instant. This ability is vital, since wild cats do not have the inexhaustible stamina of wild dogs, which sometimes track their prey for miles. Cats have to rely on a surprise attack. A healthy prey animal with quick reactions has a reasonable chance of escaping the strong jaws and sharp claws of its hunter.

All wild cats have extraordinarily well-developed senses. Many of them hunt at dusk, at night or in the early morning and their eyes are superbly adapted to these nocturnal wanderings. On a moonlit night a wild cat –and his domesticated counterpart– can see as well as they can in broad daylight. To protect their highly light-sensitive eyes against bright sunlight, cats are able to narrow their pupils to tiny slits that admit relatively little light. Cats' hearing, their strong teeth and their powerful claws are also very well-developed. The sharp claws enable cats to grasp their prey and it is therefore important that the claws should not wear down when the animal walks on hard surfaces. All the members of the cat family can consequently retract their claws to some extent.

Wild cats' coat coloration and patterning are adapted to the environment in which they live. This camouflage allows them to merge into the background so that they can get close to their prey without being seen.

The lion's sandy colouring is almost perfect camouflage against his native background

What wild cats eat

The diet of most wild cats consists of large animals like deer, gazelles, zebras and gnu. Prey of this size can provide a big cat with enough food for anything from a few days to a couple of weeks. The smaller cats tend mainly to eat rodents, rabbits, hares and reptiles, although they will also take birds and insects. They have to go out hunting more often than their larger relatives in order to catch enough for their needs.

It has been found that wild cats, unlike members of the dog family, primarily eat the soft flesh and the innards of their prey, leaving the bones, skin and other less digestible parts to the carrion eaters. Wild cats are in fact more strictly carnivorous than wild dogs, which will consume virtually every scrap of their prey.

Like wild cats, our domestic cats are able to reduce their pupils to slits and can see very well in near darkness

Solitary wild cats

Most cats are solitary. They usually have their own territory in which they will not tolerate any other member of the same species, except during the mating season. Solitary cats mark the boundaries of their territory with scent, so that other individuals know that they can go no further. Strategic spots are sprayed with urine or a pile of droppings is deposited as a marker. Many cats will rub the sides of their heads, which contain scent glands, against specific objects, or leave claw marks on the trunks of trees.

Domestic cats really differ very little from their wild cousins in this respect. Our pets also have their own territories, which they can mark in the same ways. Other cats will usually respect these boundaries and things seldom end in conflict.

The Tiger

The size of a tiger's territory is directly related to the number of available prey animals. In some areas, where there is plenty of game, a tiger (*Panthera tigris*) can survive in a territory of ten square miles or even less, but tigers have also been found to cover a territory of a couple of hundred square miles.

The Sumatran tiger looks very impressive, but is actually one of the smallest tigers there is

Tigers are the largest and most dangerous of the big cats, but they are also the most beautiful and impressive

Tigers generally produce two or three cubs, who may well stay with their mother for two years or more. There are various species of tiger. The best-known and the largest of all is the Siberian tiger. Males of this rare species can weigh over three hundred kilos (around seven hundred pounds) with an overall body length of four metres (13 feet).

In the countries where tigers are indigenous, the local people are less than happy with their presence. There are a number of reasons for this, among them the fact that tigers are the only wild cats that not infrequently prey on people as well as large animals, but chiefly because tigers will hunt even when they are not hungry. (Other big cats, including lions, only ever attack people if there is a shortage of natural prey.)

Tigers are widely feared in the areas where they occur, and this has meant that they are hunted remorselessly; some species have actually be- come extinct. Conservationists have taken up the fight on behalf of the tiger and are trying by means of research and education to prevent any more of these fascinating but dangerous animals from being shot unnecessarily. Their efforts have already met with success in some places.

In India, for example, people now wear a life-like mask of a face on the back of their heads if they have to go into an area where tigers are known to be. The idea behind this is that a tiger only ever attacks its prey from behind. By wearing a mask like this, a person can move reasonably safely through the forest. The tiger leaves masked people alone because he cannot find the back of the prey in order to mount his attack.

The Puma

Pumas (also known as cougars) likewise live and hunt alone, both at night and during the day.

They are found in the United States and else-where. When these animals succeed in killing a large prey, they hide it under a thick covering of leaves to throw any scavengers off the scent. The puma will be able to live on the contents of his larder for a week or two, and during this time he will not attack any other animals since pumas only hunt when they are hungry.

Pumas were decidedly unpopular with American farmers since they not infrequently took horses and other livestock. For years the farmers attempted to wipe out the puma by hunting it and by putting out poisoned meat in areas where pumas had been sighted.
Fortunately their efforts were not entirely successful, although the population of pumas living in the wild has fallen dramatically.

The Lynx

The lynx is another of the cats with a territory of its own. The size of the territory depends on

There are many different species of lynx and their range is enormous

how much food it contains and the species. There are several types of lynx, including the caracal, the red lynx, the North American lynx and the rare Spanish lynx.
The Siberian lynx is the largest. This animal lives in the vast Siberian pine forests and preys almost exclusively on larger animals such as deer and young wild pigs. The various species of lynx cover a vast range.
As well as in Siberia, they are found in Canada and the United States, and in parts of Europe, Asia and Africa. In Europe, lynxes effectively died out at the beginning of the twentieth century.
A few de-cades ago, projects were set up to reintroduce the lynx to its original habitats. These projects were welcomed by conservationists, but not by the Swiss, French and Italian farmers who depended for their livelihood on the meat, milk and hides from their cattle.
Despite all the furore, the lynx has reestablished itself in its former haunts in the Alps and

The Asiatic leopard cat is about the same size as a domestic cat

the project, which attracted a great deal of publi-city, can be counted a success.

The Asiatic Leopard Cat

The Asiatic leopard cat also has an extraordinarily large range. This small wild cat can be found in China, Indonesia, Pakistan and Tibet. There are many different species of Asiatic leopard cats; those that live in cold, mountainous areas have longer coats than the forest-dwellers.

One remarkable characteristic of the Asiatic leopard cat is that it loves swimming. Its prey consequently includes fish, as well as rodents and reptiles. Most leopard cats have a striking pattern of spots and streaks, but there are also completely black varieties. There are very few wild cats with completely black coats – the panther is another. Asiatic leopard cats have been imported into Western countries, particularly the United States, where they have been used in breeding programmes with domestic cats.

The Asiatic leopard cat is relatively small, weighing only three to seven kilos (seven to 16 pounds) on average - much the same size as the domestic cat.

The Panther or Leopard

The range of the panther -or the leopard- covers most of Africa, India and Southeast Asia, and parts of the Middle East. These magnificent creatures are found in the densest jungles and in desert regions. Their diet consists primarily of larger prey animals like antelopes and wild pigs, but they will also take smaller prey and in times of scarcity will even eat insects.

There are many different types of panther, among them the jaguar. The jaguar is one of the biggest species of panther and also the one that is under the greatest threat.

Males can weigh more than eighty kilos (180 pounds) at a length of one and a half metres (five feet). These superb beasts do not hesitate to attack quite large prey, but occasionally will

An Asiatic leopard cat with her young

Jaguar

Jungle cat

content themselves with a hare or a waterfowl. Numbers in the wild are declining fast as a result of hunting. Their beautiful skins are sold to the fur trade. They were placed on the list of protected species some time ago, but so far there has been no significant increase in their numbers.

Jungle cats

Jungle cats are found in regions as far apart as

Panthers -or leopards- have a very wide range

India and China, Europe and Egypt. They do not appear to have a preference for a particular type of habitat.

These wild cats live in densely forested areas and on great, open plains. They are rarely found in trees, preferring to stay on the ground, where they hunt smaller rodents, reptiles and birds. Jungle cats vary enormously in size, apparently depending on where they live.

There are, for example, jungle cats weighing around five kilos (eleven pounds), but individuals weighing as much as fifteen or sixteen kilos (33 to 35 pounds) are by no means exceptional. Some naturalists believe that this animal is one of the ancestors of our domestic cat, but this has not been proved beyond doubt. These cats are found in zoos everywhere nowadays, but their numbers in the wild have fallen dramatically.

Wild cats that live in groups

As we have seen, almost all members of the cat family are solitary. The only time they will tolerate another individual of the same species in their territory is during the mating season. The most obvious exceptions to this are lions and cheetahs, which live and hunt together in groups very effectively..

The lion

Lions are found in Africa and some protected areas in Asia. They live in groups of anything from four to as many as thirty animals, known as prides. Most of the individuals in the pride will be females. They are fairly large predators, weighing between 130 and 200 kilos (290 to 440 pounds) on average, although some males may weigh as much as 250 kilos (550 pounds). Lions live on open plains, which afford little shelter or protection. With their unmarked, sandy-coloured coats they merge into the dry, barren landscape in which they live. They prey on large animals like zebras, gazelles and gnus, but they are not above stealing food that other predators have killed.

Lions hunt in groups. It is the lionesses who do the hard work – the males, impressive as they may look, seldom soil their paws on catching and killing prey. The lionesses are almost always related to one another and it is only rarely that a strange lioness is accepted into an

It is usually the lionesses who go hunting

The lion is native to Africa, but this pride obviously feels very much at home in the zoo

Most cats are safer in the zoo than in their natural environment

Lions and tigers are the largest of the big cats

existing pride. The lionesses take joint responsibility for raising the cubs; if a lioness dies, the others will take over the care of her young. Males learn at a much later age, sometimes not until they are as much as four years old, how to hunt effectively.

Small wild cats are sometimes bought as pets, but once they grow up it is impossible to keep them in the house

This means it is very important for them to remain with the pride they were born into for as long as possible; usually, however, they are driven out at a fairly young age. These solitary males sometimes form a close-knit group with other rejected males since their chances of survival are much better if they stick together. A pride of bachelors like this generally does not remain intact for very long. Their instincts drive the males to make regular attempts to take over the leadership of prides which do contain lionesses.

In the heat of the battle, the survival of the fittest prevails and the former comradeship soon disintegrates.

The cheetah

Cheetahs are a separate group within the cat family. Their streamlined build and strong muscles make them the fastest land mammals in the world. This enables them to catch and kill their fleeing prey, usually a gazelle.

The speed of these animals can achieve during a chase is so great that they are very seldom unsuccessful, unlike most of the other, slower wild cats, which not infrequently fail to catch

The Bengal is an American cat breed, hybridized from crosses between domestic cats and Asiatic leopard cats

their prey. Female cheetahs generally live alone, although their territories may overlap without their coming to blows.

The males, in contrast, usually live in small groups and together defend the territory in which they live and hunt.

Wild cats as pets

The beauty and elusiveness of wild cats has intrigued people throughout the ages. This fascination can sometimes take extreme forms. Some lovers of wild cats are not content to watch these animals in the wild or in the zoo. They try to acquire a young animal in order to tame it and keep it as a pet. This is against the law in many countries, which is all to the good because keeping an animal like this usually ends in disappointment.

Wild cats have a deep-rooted instinct, which becomes stronger and stronger the older the animal gets. Most of them are extremely strong and can do a great deal of damage if they are not handled with the utmost care and expertise.

Keeping a wild cat as a pet is a perilous undertaking that is doomed to failure. The fact that many people, despite all the unhappy experiences of others, still want to own a cat that looks like a wild cat, has led breeders to find out whether it is possible to cross wild cats with domestic cats. It was hoped that these crosses would produce cats with the looks of a wild cat and the affectionate, home-loving character of the domestic cat.

These experiments were usually abandoned at an early stage because it became clear that, biologically, most species of wild cat could not be crossed with domestic cats. When crosses did succeed, the kittens were either not viable or turned out to be sterile.

One attempt, however, can be described as a major success. This was the programme to cross the domestic cat with *Felix bengalensis* or the Asiatic leopard cat.

Bengal kittens

The kittens from these crosses not only survived, but all the females were fertile. These crosses produced a new breed of cats, known as the Bengal.

Cats of this breed look very much like their wild ancestor, the Asiatic leopard cat, but they have a much more equable temperament.

Cats inspect their territory every day

CHAPTER 2

The history of the cat

The cat has made an indelible impression on man throughout history. In ancient Egypt cats were worshipped as gods, whereas a cat unfortunate enough to be born in Europe during the Middle Ages was denounced as a servant of the devil and treated accordingly.

Maine Coon kitten

Right: a Bengal out hunting

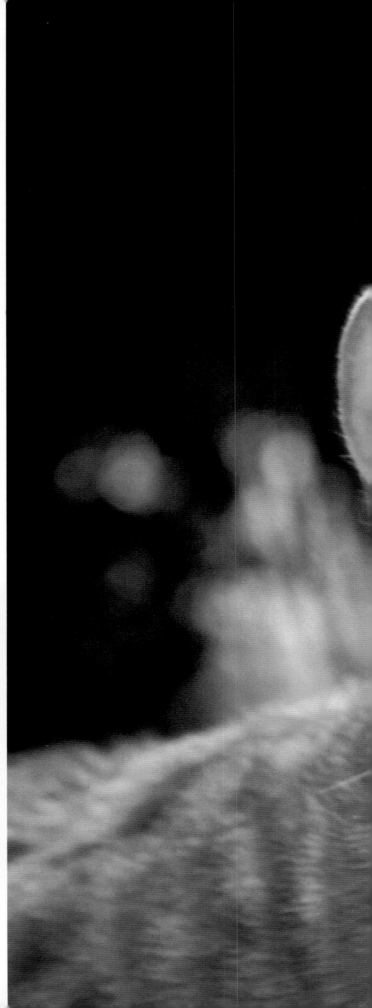

Ancient Egypt

The earliest irrefutable evidence of cats being kept as domestic pets dates from ancient Egypt around 2000 BC. Archaeological excavations have revealed countless papyrus scrolls, statues, tomb paintings and amulets with images of cats. These finds have enabled archaeologists to say with great certainty that the ancient Egyptians not only kept cats as pets, but also accorded them great religious significance.

They took their reverence for everything feline to such lengths that the women used cosmetics in an effort to make themselves look as much like cats as possible. In ancient Egypt anyone who killed a cat, whether deliberately or by accident, was irrevocably sentenced to death. It

In the Middle Ages, black cats were regarded as the servants of the devil

The Egyptian Mau is one of the oldest known breeds of cat

was also strictly forbidden to export cats to other countries. When a domestic cat died, the Egyptians observed a period of mourning and shaved off their eyebrows. Dead cats were mummified and buried with great ceremony. Archaeologists frequently come across jewelled caskets containing mummified cats, gold objects and mummified mice.

The Egyptians were evidently convinced that animals, like people, would live on in the afterlife. Sadly, a great deal of valuable information has been lost because some of the people who made the discoveries were unaware of the great archaeological significance of their finds.

A distressing but telling example of this ignorance was the party of British archaeologists at the beginning of the twentieth century,

The Abyssinian is probably a direct descendant of the cats of Ancient Egypt

who discovered a huge burial ground containing the mummified bodies of hundreds of thousands of cats. The remains were taken back to England by the shipload, where they were ground down to make fertilizer and spread on the fields. Such mass desecration must have had many an ancient Egyptian turning in his grave.

The Middle Ages

In Europe, small domestic cats were not regarded as pets; their popularity came primarily from the fact that they were excellent pest exterminators. In rural areas, in particular, cats were highly valued because they kept food stores, barns and houses free of mice and rats.

Bringing about the death of a cat did not, it is true, result in the death penalty as it did in ancient Egypt, but the perpetrator did have to recompense the owner by giving him food or some other gift. The rise of Christianity in large parts of Europe unfortunately put an end to the privileged position enjoyed by the cat.

A very sorry episode in the history of cats set in during the Middle Ages and continued in some areas until well into the eighteenth century. This was the era in which people were convinced that all evil emanated directly from the devil.

The cat, who was regarded as the servant of the devil, became the victim of this mass hysteria. According to the religious and the superstitious, it was the cat, acting on Satan's orders, that made the crops fail, spread diseases and caused other disasters of all kinds.

It was believed that the cats were aided and abetted in their evil work by witches – women who lived among the rest of the population, but whose lifestyle was unusual for the times. Fuelled by the clerics, the fear of cats and witches grew by the day not only among the superstitious and ill-educated but also in well-to-do circles.

Black cats were particularly suspect. Not a day passed without witches being tried - and persecuted - somewhere in Europe. People also proved extremely inventive in torturing cats

Although it is hundreds of years since black cats were thought to be bringers of evil, there are still people today who are afraid of black cats

and putting them on trial. Not infrequently they were put into sacks or cages and thrown on to the bonfire, and they were tortured and tormented in all sorts of unimaginable ways before death brought the wretched animals a merciful release from their suffering.

The rage against cats was probably one reason why the dreaded Black Death, a contagious disease transmitted primarily by rats, claimed so many human victims during these dark times. It is interesting to note that in the same period the Celts in Ireland, the Scandinavians and, later, the emigrants to America, were not swept up in the anti-cat hysteria.

The result was that the plague was far less widespread – or actually absent altogether – in these countries.

The rest of the world

In the history of the domestic cat it was only in certain parts of Europe that cats were subjected to mass persecution. Cats in other areas had a much better time of it. In some countries - Japan, for example - they were revered or seen as the bringers of good fortune, while elsewhere in the world they were tolerated because they were useful. In some countries their usefulness was significantly exaggerated.

In parts of the orient, people were convinced that a cat that was carried around a just-sown field and then submerged in water could make the rains come so that the seeds would germinate. The Chinese have never held dogs in very high esteem, but the cat has always been

Tri-coloured cats, known as 'Mi-Ke', are considered to be lucky in Japan

British Shorthair kitten

Cats specialize in hunting mice and other vermin

valued in China. If a Chinese kills or eats a cat, he knows that the gods will eventually punish him for his repugnant act.

In China cats are kept exclusively as mousers; a cat as a pet is unheard of and they are never cuddled or stroked. A few decades ago, the Chinese started using pesticides on a large scale to eradicate the overpopulation of vermin. The cats who ate the poisoned mice did not survive and in consequence there are very few cats in China today.

In certain parts of China a cat is worth the equivalent of three months' pay, so that the breeding – and stealing – of cats has become a very lucrative business.

From mouser to pedigree cat

The earliest recorded pedigree cats are the Turkish Angoras. As early as the seventeenth century, Italian merchants brought back white cats with a longish, silky coat from the region of Turkey.

These animals, with their blue eyes and elegant lines, bore little resemblance to the usual

Cats have a highly-developed hunting instinct. This blue British Shorthair can amuse himself for hours with a toy mouse

spices and other novelties back to Europe, they also carried unusual plants and animals. On the other side of the world, travellers encountered cats that were nothing like any cat they had ever seen at home. They took them back home and gave them to their wives, who fell head over heels in love with them. This is how the first Siamese and the Abyssinian arrived in Europe.

These cats were generally owned by women who had the time, their husband's money and the opportunity to lavish care on these animals, which often had problems adapting to the colder climate.

Whole areas, heated with the best means available, were built especially to house these creatures, and the decor of the earliest catteries

The first Siamese that were imported looked like this

Originally, white was the only recognized colour for the Turkish Angora, but nowadays they are bred in many colours

European short-haired farm cats that made themselves useful keeping down the rats and mice in grain stores and barns.

Within a very short time the Angoras, whose name was derived from the Turkish capital Ankara, became immensely popular among the wealthier Europeans and were particular favourites at the French court. It was the end of the nineteenth century before these cats, which were extremely costly at this time, were joined by other foreign breeds.

During this period the Europeans' trade with far-flung lands flourished as never before. The merchant vessels brought not only exotic herbs,

The Angora, or Turkish Angora, was a favourite at the French Court

Cats are excellent hunters and are perfectly capable of fending for themselves

included native trees and plants imported from the cats' countries of origin.

Cat shows around the turn of the century

Cat-lovers started to share their experiences by means of small periodicals. They kept one another informed of the fate of their cats,

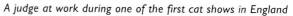

Harrison Weir, a leading member of the cat fancy

With their exotic looks, the first Siamese attracted a great deal of attention in Victorian England

A judge at work during one of the first cat shows in England

A cat show around the turn of the century

Around 1900, cat shows were the province of the wealthy and high-born

which they had meanwhile started breeding. As time passed, the Victorian nobility and the well-to-do wanted to compare their exotic cats and the phenomenon of the cat show was born. The first major cat show was organized by a well-known, leading cat fancier named Harrison Weir. This show took place at London's Crystal Palace in July 1871. Since then the 'cat fancy' – the keeping, breeding and showing of cats – has spread all over the world. Although started as a hobby by a handful of wealthy and often aristocratic Europeans, the keeping and breeding of pedigree cats is no longer a matter of status.

There are cat lovers and breeders in every part of society virtually everywhere in the world, and given the growing interest in pedigree cats, their numbers are bound to increase.

A Victorian lady with her pride and joy

CHAPTER 3

Feline behaviour

Cats are still largely an enigma to us, but scientists have been able to explain some of their behaviour.

Right: by displaying his tummy, the cat shows that he trusts us completely

Cats and people

Everyone has probably heard it said that cats born and raised in the wild can never settle to a life as a pet. Attempts to tame a feral cat are always doomed to failure. At best, the cat will remain in the neighbourhood of the house and will even come indoors to eat, but it will never learn to trust people let alone allow itself to be stroked or picked up. Why is this? Feral cats grow up without any contact with people. If there are people around, the watchful mother cat will take care to keep her kittens out of sight until the coast is clear again.

The young animals are not used to people and their mother teaches them to stand on their own four paws so that they can look after themselves when the time comes. And people, so they learn from the mother's behaviour, are creatures to be avoided. A very young kitten is still open to new impressions and impulses, but as he gets a bit older he will have absorbed all his mother's lessons and will not come up with new ideas of his own. The young cat can learn from his experiences, but the fear of people is buried irretrievably deep in his being. These cats have developed into independent feral cats. They do not need people, and have learned to look after themselves.

Our dependent pet cats, who stretch out on our laps in the evening and pester us vocally for food, are very different in character, but then they have had a very different primary edu-

Two cats get acquainted

cation. The domestic cat's kittens have been aware of the presence of humans from the moment they are born.

The mother will undertake a significant proportion of the care of the kittens herself, but at a certain point humans will take over from her. The kittens are stroked, cuddled, their coats are brushed and they are fed on time. With all this wonderful care, we are unconsciously imitating the behaviour of the mother cat.

The difference is that we do not leave the kittens to fend for themselves when the time is ripe, as a sensible feral mother cat will do; instead we continue to cosset them for the rest of their lives. In so doing we interrupt the normal, fairly rapid development from depen-

Right: children have to be taught to respect the cat

Because we look after our pets so well, the cat never outgrows the kitten stage

This Scottish Fold is grooming her kitten

The cat has an excellent sense of smell

dent kitten to independent adult cat. Our adult pet cats are all, without exception, cats who are mentally still kittens. We have taken the place of the mother, and the cat behaves accordingly. Outside the house cats do, it is true, lead a different and relatively adult life, but at home they allow themselves to be indulged by their surrogate mother.

A very obvious example of dependent kittenish behaviour is the 'kneading' that some cats do when they are happily curled up on a comfortable lap. They make rhythmic kneading movements with their forepaws and some of them will suck noisily at their owner's jumper or drool copiously. What they are doing is behaving exactly like a kitten feeding from its mother and feeling safe and protected by her presence. Kittens that are taken away from their mothers too early are likely to display this behaviour more often and more obviously than other cats.

Cats and children

It is generally accepted that cats can make a positive contribution to a child's overall development.

Children can play with cats, stroke them and cuddle them, and learn how to look after them. In the end, a placid, gentle cat will become a

The size of the territory depends on a number of factors

trusted companion with whom the child can share all his problems and secrets. The child and the cat have to learn respect for each other. The cat should never scratch or even attack the child, and the child must not be allowed to pester the cat beyond endurance or force it to do things it does not want to do.

The parents have a very important role to play here; they must teach the child what is allowed and what is not, and rebuke the cat if it behaves in an unfriendly way.

Some people are afraid that cats can give their children diseases. Of course cats can and do become ill, there is nothing surprising in that, but fortunately there are very few feline diseases or disorders can be transmitted to humans. What we must be on our guard against is a worm infestation. A cat with worms can infect a child. However, if your pet cat is wormed regularly the risk of it infecting your child is effectively ruled out.

Cats and babies

One sometimes hears of women trying to find a new home for their cat because they are pregnant. Well-meaning but ill-informed people warn pregnant women about the risk the cat poses to their unborn child. And then family and friends start advising the expectant mother to get rid of the cat for the good of the baby. This has led many young mothers-to-be to part with their beloved pets, only to find out later that there was absolutely no need for it. Because of the danger of toxoplasmosis, which can occur in cat faeces, a pregnant woman should not clean out the litter tray and she should also be careful in handling kittens. However, toxoplasmosis is also found in the soil in the vegetable patch, and eating partially cooked meat, such as a rare steak, poses the same risk.

Once the baby has arrived, the cat may be irresistibly drawn to the deliciously-smelling comfort of the crib. This is the only reason why a cat would ever try to sleep in the baby's cot -

certainly not out of jealousy or a desire to smother the little mite. The risk of a cat's actually lying on a baby is very remote, but even so it is a sensible precaution to keep the cat out of the baby's room and never leave a baby alone with a cat. Cats are no exception in this respect, since the rule applies to all pets.

The territory

Like the wild cats, the domestic cat has a territory. The territory of a neutered pet cat may be quite small, but farm toms may have a territory covering several square miles. The borders of the territory are patrolled and inspected every day.

The cat sniffs all around to find out what has been happening in the territory during his or

Cats like a good vantage point

her absence, often using a special set of receptor cells (Jacobson's organ) in the roof of the mouth, producing the characteristic grimace with the mouth slightly open known as the flehmen reaction. The round of inspection is carried out every day, usually at roughly the same time.

Other cats know exactly where the boundaries of the territory lie because they are clearly marked, and they take care not to cross them. Entire males mark by spraying urine, and they also strop their claws at strategic points. The cat will also say 'this is mine, this is my territory' by rubbing his head against objects. There are scent glands at the side of the head, and rubbing up against something releases a scent that provides a clear signal to other cats. When cats rub up against the people they live with they are actually saying the same thing – you belong to me.

Cats that never go outside regard the house they live in as their territory and mark it too. The most innocent method of marking, rubbing with the head, is often seen in domestic cats, but scratching is another entirely natural and normal form of behaviour that can sometimes be a source of annoyance to owners. If you see to it that the cat has a scratching post or a sisal or coconut matting doormat to scratch, he will usually leave the furniture alone.

A less innocent form of marking around the house is spraying. The cat turns his back on the object he wants to mark, tramples up and down with his back feet a couple of times, points his tail (usually quivering) straight up and squirts a stream of odorous urine almost horizontally at his target. Almost all toms will do this, and this is why most toms are castrated as soon as they become sexually mature. A less widely known fact is that some unneutered females will also do this, particularly when they are in season. And there are other ways in which cats, whether neutered or not, mark their territory.

This behaviour can sometimes be observed when a new pet is introduced into the household or there is some change in the make-up of the family. Some cats are so attached to their territory and their people that they will not tolerate any other pets, and they react to an intruder by urinating all over the house and even defecating in conspicuous places. Cats that do this can drive their owners to despair. Cats' faeces and, even more, their urine have a particularly pungent odour that can be extremely difficult to eradicate.

It may sometimes help to board the cat elsewhere for a long weekend, clean the whole house from top to bottom, move all the furniture around and endeavour in any other way you can think of to change the territory so that the cat no longer recognizes it.

It is absolutely essential to ensure that the marked places are completely odour-free. After his weekend away the cat may, sometimes, accept the new pet because his territory has become less recognizable. You should be aware, however, that this does not always work.

The cat, a solitary animal?

Through the ages, the domestic cat has acquired a label as a 'solitary animal', and many people get a cat as a pet even though they are out at work all day. Cats kept like this can sometimes pine away or develop maladjusted and even aggressive behaviour patterns because

Cats often love to curl up together, like these Burmese and Tonkinese

This large group of cats eats together without conflict

they are not raised to cope with loneliness. The reason for this is that our domestic cat has not developed fully into a wild, and hence solitary, creature, but has remained hung up in the kitten stage.

A kitten needs the contact with his litter brothers and sisters and with his mother, and a strong need to feel safe and protected. Most domestic cats therefore tend to get on reasonably well or very well with other cats and are happy to have a companion. This is not always the case, however. Some cats who have had 'their' house – their territory in other words – to themselves for years will not take kindly to the introduction of a pushy newcomer in the shape of another cat. These cats evidently receive enough attention and have all the social contacts they need. The reactions to the intruder can range from behavioural changes to continual savage attacks.

It does not necessarily matter whether the newcomer is a kitten or an adult cat and the sex, provided that both cats are neutered, will probably not make any difference either. Cats have their likes and dislikes, and the characters may be attractive to each other or precisely the opposite. Some breeds are outstanding in terms of their social behaviour, with the prime examples being Siamese and Oriental Shorthairs. These elegant creatures usually accept newcomers without a murmur and often go so far as to curl up and sleep together in a cosy heap.

The social behaviour of feral cats

The feral cats we sadly see all too often in large cities are rather less responsive to other cats than our domestic pets are. While it is true that feral cats are comparable to our domestic cats, they differ in that they have developed not only physically, but also mentally, into independent, adult wild cats. They have their own territories, small though these may be, and they will not usually tolerate any other cats in them.

Despite this, researchers all over the world have observed that these cats do seek one another out every once in a while. A group of cats will lie or sit together and look equally around at one another.

No displays of power, no conflicts. Cats that would normally fly at each other's throats

Cats like the Oriental Shorthair need company, so it is better to have two if you are out a lot of the time

should they come across each other close to the territorial boundaries sit together amicably. A gathering like this can sometimes last for several hours, after which the cats separate and go their own ways again.

No one has yet come up with an explanation for this extraordinary phenomenon, and no one knows what purpose these meetings serve. This is one of the many unsolved mysteries that surround the cat.

Behaviour towards other animals

Their hunting instinct means that cats are not always the best pets for people who already keep caged birds, small mammals or fish. It depends very much on the temperament of the

Oriental Longhair with two Great Danes

These two kittens are very inquisitive

Dogs and cats are not always good friends

This bunch have all found something to interest them: what is going on out there?

cat. There are cats who live all their lives in households with birds, fish, rabbits or hamsters and never give them a second glance, but there are others who are extremely ingenious and devote all their energies to opening cages or getting the covers off aquariums. This does not mean that someone who loves other small pets cannot have a cat. What it does mean, however, is that he would need to know the cat's temperament and never leave it alone with a pet that would normally be its natural prey. Cats and dogs do not always get on well together, but there are frequent instances of dogs and cats that become inseparable friends. There are bitches who go so far as to help a queen look after her litter, and there are dogs who will spring to 'their' cat's defence outside the house, if it is threatened by another cat or dog. Again, whether or not your dog and cat become friends depends on a number of factors. Success hinges chiefly on the extent to which the dog is socialized and the way the two species are introduced to each other. It will also depend on the personal character of the animals – they may take a liking to each other or hate each other on sight.

Dogs and cats speak different languages, and certain canine behaviours mean precisely the opposite in cat language. It is not surprising that communication between the two species is not always successful.

Generally speaking a puppy will learn to interpret the meaning of your cat's behaviour and a kitten that of a dog, but there are also dogs and cats who have come to live in the same house as adult animals and cohabit in perfect harmony.

Hunting instinct

Our cat is a predator. It is designed for hunting and killing prey. Fluttering birds, scurrying mice and buzzing bluebottles are irresistible stimuli that urge the cat into instinctive action. Hungry cats catch their prey quickly, kill it and eat it.

Well-fed domestic cats who really cannot be hungry delay killing their prey for a very long time. They will sometimes play with it for hours on end. As long as the mouse or fly keeps still, the cat will not touch it, but it will pounce as soon as the unfortunate creature tries to make a dash for safety.

A cat can amuse itself like this for hours and it can appear to us to be unutterably cruel. Can there be a single cat owner who has not rescued a half-dead bird from the jaws of their

The hunting instinct is deeply rooted in every cat

Left: a toy in the form of a fur mouse brings all the cat's hunting instinct to the fore. A toy like this can be the ideal solution for 'solitary' cats

beloved pet and attempted to return it to the wild? We feel really angry when our pet comes in triumphantly carrying his prey.

It helps to know that birds account for only a tiny fraction of the domestic cat's prey and that the vast majority of it is vermin or insects. Young birds are often at far greater danger from crows, rooks and magpies – notorious nest-robbers all. A well-fed cat will not give up hunting, because it is his instinct to hunt, so there is absolutely no point in trying to punish a cat for this natural behaviour. It is better to accept that this is simply the way cats are. Some cats do, however, make it very difficult for their owners by persistently presenting them with their trophies after a night's hunting. Admittedly, a row of dead mice is not the most pleasant of sights, but the cat is offering us his prey with the best of intentions. They are evidently meant as a gift. Sadly, these good intentions are not always appreciated, but it helps to know what motivates the cat to do this.

Play

Playing with a toy mouse or a ball of paper is actually the same as hunting. A moving or

These two kittens are out hunting together

Research has shown that while cats do occasionally go for birds, their menu consists primarily of mice and small rats. Even cats that are really well fed will retain their hunting instinct.

Only the bravest and hungriest of cats would attack a prey the size of this one

Following pages: Persian Longhair

rustling object is irresistibly attractive to a cat and triggers his hunting instinct. Cats who cannot find any real prey because they never go outside can be kept amused and active with a range of interesting toys. Cats who normally sleep a lot and do not get much exercise will certainly benefit from playing with a toy mouse

This cat has caught a great tit, but the cat's menu consists mainly of mice and insects

Every cat washes several times a day

or a ball with a rattle in it, since this will help prevent them from getting too fat and hence unhealthy.

There are all sorts of cat toys in the shops and one will appeal to a cat more than another. Some toys are filled with dried catnip, which many cats adore. They roll over with the toy, rub it on their faces, purring loudly, and are clearly in seventh heaven.

Cats who would not normally give a toy a second glance sometimes find the catnip variety hard to resist.

Washing

Cats are extremely fastidious animals and they spend a large part of the day grooming their coats. They generally approach the business in a set order. They use their rough tongues to clean all the areas they can reach, and then they clean the other places with their forepaws, having first licked them clean.

The cat is unable to spit out the loose hairs that come out of the coat because his tongue is covered with tiny, backward-facing hooks. The cat consequently has no choice, he has to swallow all the loose hairs that come out during grooming. The hair forms a hairball in the animal's stomach. The size of the hairball may be anything from quite small to very large, and the cat will probably vomit it up from time to time.

There is no set pattern in the frequency with which hairballs are produced. There are cats that never vomit up a hairball in their lives – the hair passes through in the faeces – and others that do it as regularly as clockwork. People seeing this for the first time may find it an upsetting sight, but it is completely natural and nothing to worry about. It only becomes a problem if the cat ingests too much hair and a

By hissing a cat tries to keep his attacker at a distance

Pure white domestic cat

Young male Maine Coon

Birman kitten

large hairball accumulates. In some cases the hairball cannot leave the body in the natural way. Obviously this situation is to be avoided, and the way to do this is to brush and comb your cat regularly. All the hair that you remove from the cat's coat is hair that will not get into

Siamese

Grass

Many people believe that cats eat grass when they have a hairball or feel unwell, but this is not the only reason for this feline behaviour. In all probability, the main reason cats eat grass is because it contains folic acid, a vitamin which cats must have. An indoor cat will soon start chewing on the house plants in an attempt to get this essential nutrient. However, many house plants are poisonous so you should ensure that your cat always has access to a pot of freshly grown grass.

Right: Persian

its stomach when it washes. Keeping the coat clean is only one of the reasons why a cat washes.

They also lick themselves to cool down when they are too hot, or to compose themselves and recover their dignity. Any cat owner will have seen their cat wash assiduously if it has lost its footing or when it has just escaped from an awkward situation.

There are various reasons for eating grass

CHAPTER 4

Choosing a cat

As soon as we decide we want to get a cat, we are faced with a variety of questions. Should it be a pedigree cat or not? Would it be better to get a male or a female, and does it matter if the animal is older? Moggy or pedigree, expectations are always high. The new member of the household should be healthy, lovable and affectionate, and if possible should be attractive too. Some of these factors are determined genetically, while some depend on the way the kittens are raised. In this chapter, we look at all the issues involved in getting a cat.

The relationship with other pets should not present a problem

Maine Coon

Pedigree or non-pedigree?

Non-pedigree cats, also sometimes referred to as moggies, are by far the largest group among domestic cats. They are second to none in terms of unaffected beauty and affection. Most of them are short-haired and they occur in a wide range of colours and coat patterns. Their forebears may without exception have been ordinary moggies, but some of them display characteristics typical of a particular breed. Every so often they surprise us by producing long-haired kittens or kittens with Siamese markings.

This is perfectly possible, since a non-pedigree cat is the offspring of a colourful mix of animals of unknown parentage, and the input of a pedigree cat somewhere back up the family tree is by no means impossible. Non-pedigree cats are usually free, or sold for a nominal amount. The disadvantage of a cat like this is that you cannot tell in advance what it will look like as an adult – nor can you get any idea of its character, which is largely genetically determined.

This means that the chances of your dear little kitten growing up into a good-natured and affectionate cat do not depend entirely on your own efforts. Unfortunately, not all moggies are born in domestic surroundings.

They may came from a remote farm or one of many other places where the young animals have little if any contact with humans. This can make them wary and withdrawn for the rest of their lives.

If you have a clear idea about what you want in your cat – coat length, colour, character – you almost inevitably have to go for a recognized breed. With a pedigree cat, genetic factors are largely known.

The breeder knows the parent cats and in most cases the preceding generations too. This means that when you buy a pedigree cat you are less likely to be in for a surprise later in terms of its looks and character than you are if you take on a moggy. Another advantage is that most breeders are sensible enough to raise the kittens in the house, so that they are used to

The parentage of this rescue cat is obscure, but that does not make him any less special

Kittens have to learn to obey the rules

human company. Before you acquire a pedigree cat, whether it is a kitten or an adult cat, it is a good idea to find out more about the breed. Although breed-related characteristics are not as diverse as they are in dogs, they do nonetheless exist, and a little research will soon reveal that one breed appeals more to you than another.

There are breeds that are known for their placid natures, but there are others that remain active and playful to the end of their days. And then there are the talkative breeds and the ones that tend to be quieter. The price of a pedigree cat depends not only on the breed, because some breeds are more expensive than others, but also on the quality of the individual cat. A kitten that is already showing potential for a promising career in the show ring will cost a lot more than his litter brother who has 'faults' that automatically rule him out of the big prizes. These cats, usually referred to as pet quality

Foreign shorthair female on heat

cats, are generally sold to people who have no aspirations in the cat show world. In many cases, the new owner will have to sign an undertaking to have the cat neutered when the time comes and the pedigree certificate will be endorsed 'no progeny to be registered'.

The differences between a good show cat and a pet quality kitten are usually so slight as to be impossible for a layman to spot. Cats like this make superb pets, and for people who want a pedigree cat but are not prepared to spend a fortune on it this is the ideal solution.

Kitten or adult cat?

It really makes no difference whether the new addition to your household is a kitten or an older animal. The life expectancy of the cat is anywhere from ten to seventeen years, so that you can look forward to many years of companionship even from an older cat. Older cats acclimatize to a new environment fairly quickly and the bond you establish with an older cat is as strong as that with a kitten. Of course, it is great fun to watch a kitten growing up.

Young kittens are very playful and can have you in fits of laughter with their antics. But you should remember that this period lasts for a

Older cats usually settle down very well in a new environment with new people

very short time. If the age of your new pet is not particularly important to you, it is well worth considering getting an older animal. Kittens – whether or not they are a recognized breed – usually find a home quickly, but sadly this cannot be said of older cats, particularly moggies.

Most cat associations have their own rehoming service to find new homes for older pedigree

This rescue cat is perfectly happy in his new surroundings

Males are usually more placid than females

the time for it would also be wise to consider getting an older cat that has had a good foundation elsewhere.

Male or female?

The decision as to whether to have a male or female is a personal one. Once they are neutered, the character differences between the sexes are very minor, although broadly speaking males are more placid than females. Males are usually larger and sturdier than females, and as adults they have a bigger head with tomcat jowls. If you do not have definite plans to breed, you should have your cat – male or

Following pages: Birman kittens

Norwegian Forest Cat kittens

If too many kittens are born, the number of strays will go up

cats. Older common or garden cats can be found in abundance in the numerous rescue shelters. There are people who believe that rescue cats are all problem cats, but this is certainly not true. Most cats find themselves in cats' homes because of their owners' personal circumstances, such as death or divorce. What's more, many old people's homes do not allow pets.

A lot of cats who are splendid companions in every respect end up in animal shelters for this reason. There is another argument in favour of an older cat. Kittens have to be properly brought up. This does not mean teaching them to obey our commands, in the way we teach our dog. It is more a question of letting them know what we consider to be unacceptable behaviour.

A kitten will not automatically know what it is and is not allowed to do in your house, and you will have to invest time and effort in your new pet in order to train it. People who are unsure about raising a kitten or do not have

Persian Longhair kittens a few days old

If you are out a lot, it is better to get two kittens

company and if you are out of the house a lot you would do far better to get two cats so that they have some companionship. They could be two kittens from the same litter – however it must be said that this is no guarantee of a harmonious relationship once they grow up. If you already have a cat, you could consider getting a second one, although you can never be certain that the incumbent will accept the newcomer.

If your cat has been able to count on your undivided attention for years, he may well not take kindly to an interloper at first.

Right: this Border Collie and British Shorthair live together in perfect harmony

A litter of kittens should grow up in the house, in the midst of the family

female – neutered. There are already far too many stray cats in the world. Neutering a cat has the added advantage of making the animal much more home-loving, friendly and placid, and it also generally prevents them from spraying.

It is effectively impossible to keep a whole tom in the house because he will mark his territory with urine, which has an extremely pungent, penetrating smell. Unlike dog shows, which refuse to allow neutered animals, cat shows have special classes for neutered animals, with prizes and titles to be won. Ordinary domestic cats, neutered or otherwise, can also be entered for shows.

One cat or more?

Cats are often said to be solitary animals, but this is only partly true. Cats really do need

In any event give the cats a few months to get used to each other. It is difficult to say in advance which way it will go, but generally speaking the cats will get on together very well given time.

Do remember that two or more cats require more care and are proportionally more expensive to keep. This is not just a question of food and cat litter, there is also the expense of vet's bills, flea treatments and so forth.

Young Burmese

Getting your cat

There are also sorts of sources for obtaining a kitten or an older cat. If you are not interested in a pedigree cat, the animal shelter is the most obvious place to look. Or you may know someone locally whose cat has had kittens which are being brought up in the house. If you want a pedigree cat you should get in touch with the appropriate cat association, which will give you addresses of reputable breeders in your

The addresses and phone numbers of the breed organizations can be found in all the specialist cat magazines. Cat clubs hold shows several times a year. Breeds of every shape and colour will be on show, and you can talk to the

Longhair kitten

Right: Exotic

breeders. It is not usually a good idea to buy a kitten at a cat show, because the animals are often already under stress from the long journey and all the new experiences. It is better to make an appointment to go to the breeder's home and select your kitten there in peace and quiet.

This will also give you a good idea of the surroundings and circumstances in which your new pet has been raised.

Things to look for

You expect your future companion to grow into an affectionate, good-natured and, above all, healthy adult cat. This means you must take care when choosing a kitten, whether or not it is a pedigree cat.

Many non-pedigree kittens are taken away from the mother too early

The kitten you choose should be free of parasites, have no discharge from its eyes or nose, and should have clean ears. The area

A well cared for and hygienic cattery

Kittens are inquisitive and mischievous

Maine Coon kittens at four weeks old

around the anus should show no traces of diarrhoea, and a distended belly or bald spots in the coat are bad signs. Kittens are playful, mischievous and adventurous.

Normal, healthy kittens raised in a family situation should demonstrate all these characteristics during your visit. If the kittens are frightened or timid this can indicate an inadequate imprinting phase, an inherited character flaw or bad experiences with people. It will often be difficult or even impossible to accustom kittens like this to the normal life of a family and they will never be very affectionate. There are a number of contagious and fatal feline diseases. The best-known and most feared of these are feline leukaemia and feline Aids, neither of which can be communicated to humans.

At present, really reliable preventive vaccines against these diseases are not available everywhere, and a breeder of pedigree cats will have had the sire and queen tested for them before mating. Ask to see the relevant forms, and do not buy if the breeder cannot show them to you. Another factor is the age of the kittens. Non-pedigree kittens are often taken away from the mother as young as six weeks old, but it is generally considered better to leave them with her until they are twelve weeks. By this age, kittens should have been vaccinated against feline enteritis, feline panleucopaenia and the respiratory viral infections collectively referred to as cat flu, and they should have been wormed several times. The breeder will be able to give you the kittens' vaccination certificates showing when and with what the animals have been vaccinated.

Buying a show cat

The term show cat is perhaps an unfortunate one here, since it seems to imply that the cat is only suitable for showing. The main reason we keep cats, of course, is because we enjoy their company, and the term show cats is used to describe pedigree animals that are as close as possible to the breed standard.

This means that they can be both superb pets and have an excellent chance of a career as a show animal. If the new member of your household has to be show quality because you intend to breed a litter from it or to show it, you will have to be even more careful in making your selection.

Never choose a kitten from the first litter you see, however hard they may be to resist. Get all the information you can from the breed association or a general cat club. Go to several shows and look at the type, the colour and the coat texture of the cats that are winning their classes. Find out abut the different bloodlines in the breed and get the breed association to send you the breed standard. The breed standard is a description of what the ideal representative of the breed should look like. Understanding a breed standard takes a degree of knowledge, and they sometimes use terms that are not immediately clear to the novice. However, if you take the trouble to find out as much as you can and learn to recognize the desirable characteristics in the cats that are winning at the shows, you will have a head start on other beginners.

It would be nice if breeders could see right away which kittens will grow up to be champions, but life is never as easy as that. All a breeder can do is try to breed cats that come as close as possible to the breed standard by breeding only from outstanding cats who have already proved themselves at shows and by selecting those kittens that look promising at

Hey you, turn round if you dare!

I may be small, but you don't scare me

Persian Longhair kitten of `pet quality'. The length of the nose does not meet the breed standard, so this kitten will not get very far on the show bench

an early age. Inherited factors are not the only important aspects here – external factors like care, diet and unforeseen circumstances can also play a role.

If you approach the matter well-armed with knowledge, the chance of getting a future champion is much greater than if you trust to luck and pick a kitten simply because it appeals to you for some reason. It pays to know what you are doing if you have ambitions for your pet.

Biff!

That's shown you!

CHAPTER 5

What you need

In this chapter we look at all the things you will need to get for your cat.

A bashful Cornish Rex

Right: Birman kitten with a toy

Oriental Longhair

Litter tray

One of the first things you should get before you bring a cat or kitten into your home is a good litter tray. They are available in a range of sizes and models.

The cheapest are small, shallow open trays, which have their drawbacks compared with the more expensive, covered types. Cats instinctively bury their urine and faeces. A cover on the litter tray does help to prevent litter from flying in all directions during enthusiastic excavation work. A cover also helps to keep the penetrating smell of urine inside the tray. There are covered litter trays with odour filters and there are also models with a flap over the entrance.

These refinements reinforce the effect of the cover, and the smell that can emanate from a litter tray is reduced to the minimum. If you have several cats, you may find that you need more than one litter tray. Some cats refuse point blank to use the same tray as their companions.

Cat litter

The days when cats had to perform on sand or shredded newspaper are long gone. Over the years, all sorts of much better cat litters have appeared on the market. There are environmentally-friendly litters based on wood or paper, most of which can safely be composted after use.

There are also clay-based litters which almost immediately harden into a clump when your cat urinates. This clump is then easily removed with a plastic litter scoop. An additional advantage of these litters is that the remaining litter stays clean – the litter lasts much longer than other types and the tray stays fresh-smelling for longer. And lastly there are other types of litter that absorb urine reasonably well, but are less economical in use than the other

This blue and white Turkish Angora has found a splendid lookout post

A stainless steel food bowl

Somali

kinds because a large proportion of the litter has to be changed every day. Try various types until you find out which is the best for you. Your cat may have a decided preference for one particular type of litter.

Some cats are so attached to their familiar litter that they will not accept any other sort.

Feeding dishes

There is no need to buy expensive bowls and dishes for your cat to eat and drink from, since the cat really couldn't care less. As far as the cat is concerned, plastic dishes are fine, but so are glass and china bowls.

They do have the disadvantage of breaking if they are dropped, but on the other hand plastic bowls tend to slide around while the cat is eating.

Your pet shop will sell metal stands which hold stainless steel dishes, and while these are not

An automatic feeder

choose to sleep off the ground. Most cats will appreciate a highish sleeping place on top of a climbing post. You can also buy special hammocks to suspend from the radiator. Some cats adore them, while others simply don't want to know.

Collars and harnesses

If your cat is free-ranging, he or she really should wear a collar. If a cat is wearing a collar, it cannot possibly be mistaken for a stray, and if it has a disc with your address or telephone number on it everyone knows where the cat lives.

Do take care to use a special cat collar, which has a section of elastic in it. This is quite literally vital, because it will stretch or break if

There are all sorts of cat beds

cheap they do have some advantages. They cannot slip, they are indestructible, and they can be sterilized if necessary. You can also buy various types of automatic feeders with timers, which release fresh dry food for your cat at set intervals while you are out. There are also feeders with a silo which will hold a couple of kilos of dry food.

These silos can be very convenient if you have several cats. The silo only needs refilling when all the food has gone, but you must remember to wash it regularly. Cats are generally not messy eaters, but it does no harm to put a place mat under the cat's food and water bowls.

Beds

The cat obviously has to have its own place to sleep in the house. Pet shops sell an amazingly wide selection of beds and baskets in all shapes and sizes. Not all cats appreciate their owner's well-meaning intentions however, and far prefer to sleep in a cardboard box.

Cats like to be able to survey their surroundings from the place where they sleep and will often

Two British Shorthair kittens in a cat hammock

Below: not all cats appreciate a basket. However, this Manx seems very happy with his

it gets caught on a branch or something similar, and allow the cat to escape from it.

It may help to stop your cat from catching birds and other prey during his forays outside the house if you attach a bell to the collar, so that the prey can hear the cat coming and take evasive action. The drawback to the collar is that the fur around the neck can wear. If you ever have to take your cat out, a cat harness can be very useful.

Harnesses are made in a variety of materials, but whichever one you choose make sure it fits properly.

A well-fitting harness will stop the cat from running away in a panic, whereas a cat can usually worm its way out of a collar.

This kitten has his own luxury two-seater sofa

Below: a cat harness must always fit well

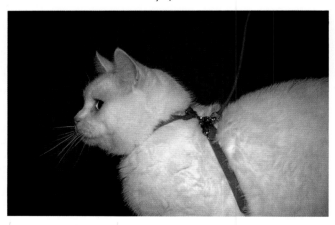

Travelling

The cat will have to be transported several times a year – to the vet's, to the cattery or perhaps to a show. There are very placid cats who will go quite happily on a harness, but these are very definitely the exception. If you are taking the cat by car and have no one to help you, it is extremely dangerous if the cat is roaming loose in the car or only on a lead. Most cats feel safe in a carrier; they will stay quiet and you can concentrate on your driving. Injured and sick cats should also always be transported in a carrier rather than on a lead. There are various types of travelling boxes for cats.

Many people find wicker baskets attractive, but the fastenings are not always reliable and they cannot be cleaned properly. A strong, not too small plastic carrier is therefore a better –and often cheaper– choice. Check when you buy that the carrier is made from sturdy material and that the fastening is not only secure but also quick and easy to open and shut.

Brushes and combs

Cats are naturally fastidious animals and they keep their own coats clean as far as they are able. However, you should help them with their

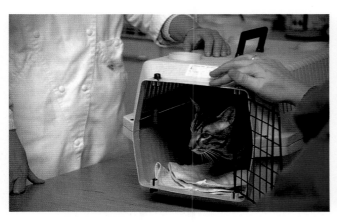

You will need a cat carrier

Cats are superb climbers, as this Siamese demonstrates

grooming every now and then. All the loose hair you brush out of the coat is hair that does not get into the cat's stomach or on to your carpets and furniture.

Each type of coat has its own specific grooming requirements. A rubber brush is ideal for removing the loose, dead hair from a very short coat, but if you use it on a long-haired cat you will find that it has very little effect.

Cream Persian Longhair kitten

Following pages: a low voltage current will keep some cats in the garden, but by no means all, as this cat demonstrates

Coarser combs and brushes with slightly stiffer bristles are suitable for long-haired cats, or you can use brushes with metal pins on an air cushion. Make sure the pins are tipped with a protective plastic coating or you could damage the animal's skin.

The one thing above all others that you must always have is a good flea comb, which you should use to check the coat for fleas once a week. Flea combs have teeth that are set very close together so that the fleas are trapped between the teeth. These combs are not easy to use on long-haired cats.

A small pair of nail scissors or clippers designed specifically for cats is also useful for snipping off the tips of your cat's claws if they get too long.

Climbing and scratching post

A good climbing and scratching post is a sound investment in several respects. Your cat will prefer to sharpen her claws on the tough sisal of the scratching post rather than on your furniture, wallpaper or doorposts.

The climbing and scratching post is used as a place to play and a larger one will become a

Cats like to sharpen their claws on mats

Right: British Shorthair, blue point kitten

Left: Scottish Fold kitten

favourite sleeping place. Scratching posts comes in all shapes and sizes. The simplest types consist of a carpeted base with a sisal-covered post screwed into it.

The most ambitious types are real cat paradises with all sorts of places to hide and play, which can accommodate several cats at a time. The one you choose depends not only on your decor, your taste and your budget, but also on the number of cats you have and whether or not your cat can go in and out of the house freely.

Cats that never go outside have to use up their energy indoors and so they need a more ambitious scratching and climbing post than their free-ranging cousins. If you have several cats, one small scratching post may sometimes be appropriated by the dominant cat and the others are left to fend for themselves. In this case you either need to buy some more small

A vantage point atop the scratching post makes an ideal place to sleep

and that there are no staples or other sharp objects sticking out. Small scratching posts are really only suitable for kittens anyway. The post should be at least as tall as the length of the cat with its forelegs and hind legs extended, and it should of course be completely stable. Sisal and coconut matting doormats are other scratching options that most cats will enjoy using frequently.

Toys

Young kittens are very playful, but many older cats love playing too. There is absolutely no need to buy your cat expensive toys to play with, unless it gives you pleasure to give your cat a treat.

Most cats will play for hours with pieces of screwed-up paper, table tennis balls and strong cardboard boxes with holes made in them here and there. In any event never give your cat toys on which he could harm himself. Unsuitable toys include twist-ties, wooden skewers, balls of wool or crumpled aluminium foil.

Cats quite often swallow wire or pieces of aluminium foil and these can cause major problems in the intestine. Sharp objects can become stuck in an overenthusiastic cat's mouth or throat.

Beads, balls that are too small and other small objects are also dangerous because the cat may

scratching posts, or else invest in a big one with a number of different levels. When buying a scratching post check that it is sturdy enough

A sturdy climbing and scratching post will give your cat hours of fun

Domestic cat

swallow them. However, most of the toys you can buy at the pet shop are quite safe. Cats can be very particular about their toys; some of them, for instance, love balls that make a noise, while others show no interest at all. Mice made of rabbit fur are also very much a question of taste. Since many cats absolutely adore the smell of catnip, a lot of manufacturers use catnip in their cat toys to increase their attraction.

Siamese

The outdoor run

There are many reason why you would be advised not to let your cat range freely out of doors. Traffic, theft and people who hate cats are the greatest threats to your pet cat. The cat can also pick up a number of potentially fatal diseases, such as feline Aids, outside. A cat catches the disease through contact with infected cats, possibly as a result of fighting or mating. Most cats really enjoy going out, and this is why most people do let them out.

There are all sorts of toys for cats

This Turkish Angora enjoys his time in the outdoor run

Birman, seal tortie point in summer coat

However, if the cat is accustomed from an early age to a life indoors, there is a good chance that later on he will have little or no interest in leaving the garden or even in going outdoors. It is perfectly possible to keep an indoor cat, but it is good for every cat to get a breath of fresh air every now and again. A cat run can be the answer. You can buy ready-made cat runs, but you can also make one yourself. If you do make your own, make sure that it is big enough and strong enough. The materials obviously need to be weatherproof and there should be no sharp edges on which your cat could hurt himself. A covered run gives the cat the opportunity to go outside even when it is raining, and if you build it so that it connects to a window or door, you won't have to keep carrying your cat to and from the run. It is a good idea to furnish an outside run with a variety of interesting things, such as a firmly anchored tree trunk or branch with the bark removed, a little drinking fountain and a couple of pots of grass you have grown from seed. In a covered run, a thick, dangling ship's rope can provide your cat with hours of fun. The space in the run can be used even more effectively if you fix up some shelves at different heights. Some people prefer to secure the whole garden so that it is extremely difficult for the cat to stray beyond its confines. Most cats will be deterred by a low voltage electric wire along the top of a fence or a high wire netting fence with the top few inches bent inwards.

The cat flap

Cat flaps are ideal if you are happy to let your cat come and go as he pleases. The simplest cat flaps can only be closed off with a shutter. There are also cat flaps with four different positions. This means that you can set the flap so that the cat can come in at night, but not go out again, or vice versa. A cat flap does, however, have one drawback: you may find yourself honoured by a visit from other cats in the neighbourhood. This is why you can now buy cat flaps that are operated by a tiny transmitter attached to the cat's collar. Although it sounds ideal, even this has its disadvantages. If your cat loses its collar outside, for instance, it could spend the night sitting outside a locked door.

Identification

Dogs are tattooed while still in the litter for identification purposes, but this is seldom done with cats. With the exception of the breeds with folded ears, they all have upright and relatively hairless ears, which means that a tattoo would be very unsightly.

Until recently, the only way to identify a cat was on the basis of its colour and any distinguishing characteristics, or by an address disc or barrel attached to its collar. In practice, neither of these 'systems' really works. There are lots of cats with the same coat colour and markings, and collars are frequently lost.

Recently, however, scientists developed a chip in which the cat's details can be stored. The data can be read with a special piece of equipment.

The chip is implanted under the cat's skin by the vet, and the cat will not even know that it is there.

Male Maine Coon

Persian Longhair, seal point

CHAPTER 6

The care of your cat

Caring for your cat means more than brushing its coat and filling its food bowl. This chapter looks at everything involved in looking after a cat.

Somali

Right: Birman

Caring for the coat

If you look after your cat's coat well, you not only cut down on the amount of hair that gets on to your clothes and your furniture, you also prevent the cat from swallowing excessive amounts of hair during his daily grooming sessions.

A short-haired cat can be groomed with a soft bristle brush and an appropriate cat comb about once a week. Cats that naturally have a sleek, glossy coat will really benefit from a gentle wipe with a slightly damp chamois leather after brushing.

If the cat is shedding so heavily that combing and brushing do not help, a special rubber brush may be the answer. The advantage of these brushes is that they are extremely efficient in removing loose, dead hair, but if you use

A well-groomed Persian is a magnificent sight

them inexpertly or too often you can pull too much hair out. Cats with moderately long coats

Maine Coon kitten

Natural breeds with semi-long coats, like this Siberian Forest Cat, need little more grooming than short-haired cats

–which means all the long-haired breeds with the exception of the Persian– need little more in the way of grooming than the short-haired breeds.

The Persian, however, is a very different matter indeed. A Persian's coat will very soon become matted and unkempt if it is not looked after properly. The condition can become so serious that the cat starts to suffer skin rashes and ultimately even abscesses. These cats must be brushed and combed thoroughly every day to prevent tangles from forming.

You should exercise a degree of caution, however, since overenthusiastic brushing and combing can pull healthy hair out of the coat and that, of course, is not the idea at all.

Show cats

If you are planning to show your cat, you will have to start by ensuring that it is in peak condition - in other words neither too thin nor too fat. The coat should look as good as possible, the ears and eyes must be clean. It is also good practice to clip off the sharp tips of the claws regularly.

Cat shows are beauty contests, and a well-groomed animal will always do better than a cat whisked straight out of the garden and off to the show. To get the coat as clean as possible you can shampoo the cat about a week before the show. Because most cats' coats take at least a week to settle down after a shampoo, there is no point in leaving it until closer to the date of the show.

When you are washing the cat, make sure water does not get into its eyes or ears and that it cannot swallow any. Always use a special cat shampoo and never one intended for humans, since the latter can cause considerable damage to the texture of the coat and the sebaceous glands in the cat's skin. You can dry the cat with a hair dryer, but if this frightens him, you can rub him dry with a towel and leave him in a warm, draught-free place to finish drying off. Some cats really dislike being bathed, but there are other ways of cleaning the coat. Short-haired cats can be given a bran bath with a generous quantity of warmed bran, which removes the dirt and excess grease from the coat.

The bran is rubbed into the coat and then brushed out almost immediately. You cannot give a long-haired cat a bran bath however, since the bran remains stuck in the animal's fur, so an unscented powder is used instead. Unneutered long-haired cats, particularly Persians, shed copiously in the spring and summer and are less attractive at this time. This is one reason why few cat shows are held

Tear marks can cause unsightly discoloration

in the summer months and why you will not see many long-haired cats at such shows as there are.

The care of the eyes

Every cat occasionally gets some dirt in the corners of its eyes. This is easily removed with a soft, damp tissue. Flat-faced cats, like Persians and Exotics, are relatively prone to suffer from blocked tear ducts, which can cause unsightly discoloured tear marks on the face. Eye care is consequently extremely important in these two breeds.

There are special eye drops on the market for daily use, and you should also clean the skin around the eyes every day.

The care of the ears

Most cats go all their lives without suffering from any ear problems, so there is no need for preventive cleaning of the ear. If the cat has dirty ears -but not otherwise- you can massage the dirt out of the ear with ear lotion and then remove it gently with a tissue or cotton wool bud. Take great care when doing this, however, otherwise you could push the dirt further into the ear. Your cat may occasionally be troubled by ear mites. The telltale signs are particles of dark brown, offensive-smelling matter. Ear mites must always be treated otherwise they

A Persian Longhair sheds heavily in the spring

A Persian cream point tom in his summer coat

can cause a severe ear infection. Your vet will have a simple and effective remedy for ear mites available.

The care of the claws and teeth

You should check the teeth regularly for tartar, because this dark deposit on the teeth can lead to decay and ultimately to tooth loss. Try to prevent tartar build-up by given your cat hard, dry food regularly.

Some cats love chewing bones, but you should never let your cat do this because pieces of bone may become lodged in the mouth and bone splinters could damage the cat's intestines.

If your cat does have tartar, the best thing is to ask your vet to remove it. Cats shed their milk teeth between three and six months of age, and

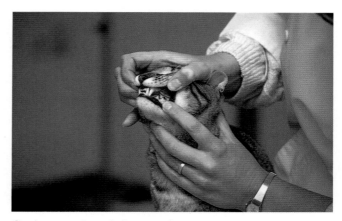

Check your cat's teeth for tartar from time to time

it is good practice to check this process every now and then. A milk tooth that refuses to come out can prevent the eruption of the permanent tooth and the teeth will develop crookedly.

This can also cause abscesses. Clip off the sharp tips of the claws regularly with good

Exotic, young black tortoiseshell female

Following pages: Foreign Shorthair, cinnamon spotted

clippers made specifically for cats or small dogs. The nail clippers we use on our own nails are not suitable since they can cause the cat's claws to split and fray.

Diet

Cats are fastidious eaters. They appear to know instinctively what is and what is not edible – there are plenty of people who get their cat to 'inspect' meat and meat products they are not sure about.

Nonetheless, we should be wary of relying on this test, because not every cat has such a superb sense of smell, and a cat's sense of smell also diminishes with age. Most cats will eat what is put in front of them, provided that the food is not tainted.

Neutered cats can develop an unattractive belly flap

Norwegian Forest Cat

There are, however, cats who are extremely faddy in their eating habits. Some will only eat a particular brand or a particular type of meat and refuse to touch anything else.

This can sometimes be the result of spoiling. The cat has learnt that he will get something better if he turns his nose up at what he has been given. Unfortunately, the alternative is not always healthier, so we should try to prevent the cat from developing these fads by feeding a variety of things, and not being too quick to put down something else if he does not like what he has been given.

The cause can sometimes be traced back to too monotonous a diet in kittenhood. Some cats are not used to different types of food and will be suspicious of anything new for the rest of their lives.

Generally speaking, a cat will not eat more than he needs, and you can leave dry food in the food bowl all day without worrying that he will eat more than is good for him. This does not, however, apply to neutered cats. They are more likely to put on weight than other cats.

A suitably modified diet and lots of exercise (play) will help to keep their weight within bounds.

Cats enjoy their food and do not like to be disturbed while they are eating. If you have a dog too, it is better to feed the cat on a raised surface so that he can eat in peace. Kittens and young cats have small stomachs, so it is better to feed them small quantities several times a day.

Types of food

Unlike dogs, cats need a great deal of high-grade animal protein. Some people make up their cat's food themselves, but this calls for a great deal of knowledge and understanding of both the cat's dietary requirements and the composition of the various ingredients and how they react with one another.

When you feed your cat commercial cat food, you know that he is getting all the correct nutrients.

There are many different types of food on the market – dry food, tinned food and frozen complete diet being the best known. The advantage of dry food is that it is relatively cheap and nutritious, and does not go off quickly.

You can leave a bowl of dry food down for your cat all day. Tinned food, on the other hand, must be eaten reasonably quickly, otherwise it is likely to go off, particularly in hot weather. Because tinned food is not as nutritious as dry, the cat needs more of it and it is relatively expensive.

Frozen complete diet comes closest to the cat's natural dietary needs and is more nutritious than tinned food, but it is more expensive and will go off quite quickly.

Young Persian Longhair

Older cats sleep more

Extras

Since a cat's digestive system is designed to cope with a very varied range of food –unlike that of the dog– you can also feed them on cooked meat or fish in addition to commercial cat food. Suitable types of meat include beef, chicken, turkey, lamb's heart and rabbit. Boned cod is a suitable fish.

Offal such as lights and tripe is less suitable for cats because the protein content is not high enough, but you can give your cat liver once a week.

Cats should never be given pork. Pork can be infected with a bacterium that causes Aujeszky's disease, which is fatal to cats. People used to believe that cats needed to drink milk, but we now know that milk is not really good for cats. Ordinary cow's milk can actually cause diarrhoea in many cats. If you want to pamper your cat every now and then, a little full-fat evaporated milk or single cream can do no harm.

The litter tray

The litter tray must be cleaned out once a day and, if several cats are using it, more often than that. Cats are extremely clean, fastidious animals, and if their tray is dirty and smelly they will go elsewhere. Many cats prefer a particular type of litter. If they find a different type in the tray they may refuse to use it. Research has shown that cats prefer a fine-grained grit, which probably has to do with the sensitive pads of their paws.

The drawback to this type of litter, however, is that the particles stick to the fur of long-haired cats. Depending on the number of cats you have, and the type and quality of litter you use, you will have to empty the tray out completely once every couple of days or once a week, disinfect it and fill it with clean grit.

Clump-forming litters last longer than other types, because the cat's urine forms into a solid clump that is easily removed with a plastic scoop. The rest of the litter usually stays dry and clean.

If you use this type of litter you can put a fairly deep layer in the tray because the urine is unlikely to reach the bottom of the tray and cause the litter to stick to it.

Parasites

There are various parasites that might trouble your cat, but the most familiar and the commonest are fleas and worms.

Fleas can drive cat and owner alike to distraction, not only because they cause the cat great irritation, but because they are extremely difficult to get rid of and multiply unbelievably fast. The flea will prefer a cat or dog as a host, but will certainly go for human blood if nothing else presents itself. Flea droppings are small, irregularly shaped blackish specks. If you find them in your cat's coat, it is probable that he has fleas.

Research has revealed that at any given time no fewer than 99 percent of fleas –in egg, larval or pupa stage– are not actually on the cat itself but in the immediate vicinity – in other words, in your home. This is why it is so important to treat not just the cat itself and any other pets, but also the surroundings. To prevent fleas from gaining the upper hand, it helps to vacuum clean a lot.

Fleas cause considerable itching and discomfort

The larvae feed on, among other things, flakes of skin on the ground. Frequent vacuuming helps to restrict their food supply. You should also spray the house regularly with a flea killer. There are all sorts of products available for treating the cat. Some work extremely well, others seem to make little difference. There are cats who are frightened by the noise of aerosols, and flea collars –like ordinary collars– have the disadvantage of damaging the fur on the cat's neck.

Generally speaking flea powder, which you can get from your vet, does the job very well. This is usually pretty strong stuff, however, so it is not advisable to use it on kittens.

The vet will have a special flea powder that is safe for kittens.

Worms, particularly roundworms, are other parasites that can make our cat's life unpleasant. All kittens are infested with worms at birth, and it makes absolutely no difference whether or not the mother cat has been wormed regularly.

Kittens must therefore be treated for worms at an early age. Preventive treatment twice a year usually provides sufficient protection for an adult cat.

Vaccinations

As long as kittens are being fed by the queen, they will be adequately protected against a number of diseases by the antibodies in her milk. Once they are weaned, however, it is time for them to be vaccinated.

Good vaccines are available against feline panleucopaenia, feline calicivirus and cat flu; it

is also possible to vaccinate against rabies and Aujezsky's disease. Cats will usually only be vaccinated against Aujeszky's disease if they regularly come into contact with pigs. In Britain, cats will only be vaccinated against rabies when they go into quarantine upon entering the country, or if they are being exported to another country where rabies is endemic. Most countries will require a rabies vaccination certificate showing that the cat has been vaccinated no longer than a year previously but also not too soon before the date of the journey. Your vet will be able to tell you what the rules are.

If your kitten has been vaccinated while it was with the breeder, you will be given a vaccination booklet showing when the kitten was vaccinated, against which diseases and with

A very old moggy

Good boarding catteries are usually fully booked long before the holiday period

Sphynx queen with her kittens

which vaccines. It will also specify when the booster vaccinations are needed. Make sure you always keep your cat's vaccinations up to date, because some diseases are fatal and there is no point in taking risks.

The sick cat

Cats are tough creatures and not particularly susceptible to illness. There are, however, inherited and contagious diseases that can affect your cat. If you buy a kitten from a good breeder, make sure it is vaccinated at the right time and care for it as well as possible, you will in any event have left nothing to chance. There are various signs which will tell you that all is not well with your cat.

Changes in behaviour, changes in eating and drinking patterns, unusual stools and difficulties passing water or stools are some of them. Discharge from the nose or eyes, and

from the vulva in a female, a visible third eyelid, skin rashes, bald patches or sudden hair loss are also signals that something is wrong, as is drooling, a distended abdomen and frequent vomiting. You know your cat: if you have the slightest doubt, contact your vet immediately.

The old cat

The average life expectancy for a cat is between ten and twelve years, but this is just an average and cats can easily reach the age of eighteen or more.

The life expectancy is partly genetically determined, but it also depends on the general health of the cat, the degree of care it receives and the quality of its diet. Statistically, a free-ranging, unneutered cat is likely to live less long than an 'indoor' cat.

In time you will notice that the cat finds it harder to hop up on to the top of the cupboard and perhaps that he is getting thinner. Because an older cat's coat does not lie as flat, it is less effective in protecting him against cold and wet. It is a good idea to keep older cats in at night to prevent them from catching cold. The sense of smell in the older cat is considerably diminished and many of them become hard of hearing.

There are even cats whose sight visibly deteriorates. Some cats start having 'accidents' because they begin to lose control of their bladders or bowels. If you put several litter trays around the house, your cat will be able to get to one more easily and the chance of accidents is reduced. There are cats who become noisier and demand more attention as they get older. Others become more withdrawn and sleep a great deal.

Older cats often have problems with their teeth; kidney problems are common, too, particularly in males. This means that an older cat will sometimes have to have a special diet. Cats who have lost some or most of their teeth do best on tinned or frozen food, but you can still feed dry food provided you soften it first in warm water or warm evaporated milk.

An older cat needs more care and attention. There will undoubtedly come a time when you ask yourself whether it would not be better for the cat to make the final trip to the vet. If you are prompted by the fact that your cat is in pain or has made it clear that he is no longer happy, in his own interests do not postpone the difficult, but only right decision for too long.

A young Norwegian Forest Cat

Exotic

Holidays

When you go on holiday you can leave your cat at home provided that you have friends or neighbours who will take care of the cat while you are away.

Cats are happiest in their own surroundings, and provided they are well looked after this is the most obvious solution. If you are unwilling or unable to leave your cat at home, you will have to find a suitable boarding cattery well before the date of your holiday.

Most reputable catteries get booked up well before the holiday period, so do not wait too long before making your reservation. Prices can vary as can the amount of space and time that is available.

If you have any special requirements –if, for example, your cat has to be given medication or needs a special diet– check beforehand to make sure that the cattery can handle this.

CHAPTER 7

The history of cat breeds

There are around seventy different breeds of cat, which can broadly be split up into three groups.
This chapter tells you about these different groups and how the various types of cats developed.

British Shorthair

Right: the classic tabby marking of this male British Shorthair makes an ideal camouflage in the bushes

The effect of mutations

All domesticated cats are descendants of *Felis domesticus*, the domestic house cat of Ancient Egypt. Scientists have still not been able to agree about which wild cat can claim to be the ancestor of this cat, but some believe it was the desert cat, a wild cat of varying size. Domestic cats were originally found only in Egypt and neighbouring regions.

The fact that we now find cats in many places all over the world is primarily a result of man's wanderlust, and man took his cats with him when he migrated elsewhere. The desert cat was –and still is, for that matter– a sand-coloured animal with a short coat, but the cats of today come in an immense variety of colours and markings, and their physical build is equally diverse.

In the orient, we find slender, svelte, smooth-haired cats, while in colder areas cats tend to be larger and sturdier, with a thicker coat. We might wonder how domestic cats today can

Manx

look so different. The answer is that all the known cat breeds are mutations. Mutations are changes in genetic material that occur spontaneously.

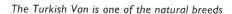

The Turkish Van is one of the natural breeds

Sokoke

Norwegian Forest Cat

Black Foreign Longhair

It is a natural phenomenon that is as old as time itself, and it is found in every type of animal, in humans and in plants. Some mutations go unnoticed. An individual is born, apparently a normal example of its species, reproduces and dies, without anyone ever suspecting that the animal or plant is a mutation.

However, mutations that cause changes in appearance will be spotted immediately. A kitten can be born, for example, with a different type of coat, a stumpy tail or short legs. Since the mutation occurs in the animal's genetic material, the characteristic can be passed on to future generations, but only if the mutant is viable and capable of reproduction. If the mutation results in a new characteristic which gives the cat an advantage over the other members of his species, it goes without saying that he and his offspring have a greater chance of survival.

The mutants then gain the upper hand over the non-mutated animals and in some cases the latter, being less well armed in the struggle for existence, eventually die out. The outcome of a mutation may not always be beneficial. Sometimes the mutation is unnecessary or even damaging, and then the mutant soon dis-

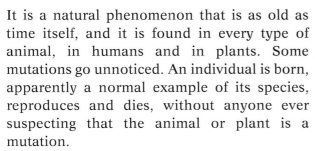

Persian Longhair

appears from the scene. Sometimes, however, the mutation reveals an indispensable characteristic which gives the species a better chance of survival in a changed situation. Since evolution never stands still, mutations still happen all the time.

Some old mutated breeds

The Siamese is a good example of a series of fortunate mutations. This cat lived in tropical regions, and obviously a cat with a smooth, sparse coat is better equipped to cope with the heat than a cat with thick fur. The Siamese's

Long-haired Dachshund and a Foreign Tabby

large ears and relatively long head meant that the cat was able to cool off quicker; what's more, cats with the Siamese markings had an advantage over other cats with tabby coats, because the light falls more directly closer to the equator, shadows are sharper and contrasts are greater. In short these variations, with which a number of mutants were born, allowed the species to survive in this area.

Another classic example is the Norwegian Forest Cat, which has a semi-long-haired, double coat that does not tangle to protect it from the severe Scandinavian winters. The cat has a long, thick, bushy tail that it can drape around itself like a blanket. Most Norwegian Forest Cats were tabbies.

This pattern provided superb camouflage in densely forested areas. If a mutant with a thin coat, big ears and Siamese markings had ever been born in the far north –and this is perfectly possible– it would have had virtually no chance of survival.

Throughout the centuries, all over the world, cat populations developed which, in terms of coat colorations and markings, the thickness of their coats and their physical build, were equipped as effectively as possible to ensure the survival of the species.

Natural breeds

By natural breeds we mean cats that appeared in significant populations long before humans started to take an interest in breeding cats. The Turkish Angora, the Manx, the Maine Coon and the Japanese Bobtail are good examples of cats that are described in old letters and appear on old prints.

The old cat breeds are now divided into natural and non-natural breeds, although one could well ask whether the term non-natural is justified here, since all cats are flesh and blood

The Turkish Van with blue eyes is quite rare

creatures and hence creations of Mother Nature.

In fact, however, the term natural breeds is used to refer to groups of cats which have developed in one way or another, without any deliberate intervention by breeders or cat fanciers, and have remained in existence down the centuries.

The aim of breeders today, as far as these natural breeds is concerned, is not to perfect or modify the type, but to maintain the original appearance of the breed.

Another factor used to make a distinction between natural breeds and other old breeds that are not considered as such, is that natural breeds can still be found today, looking just the same, in their country or region of origin. Breeders of the Manx, the Sokoke and the Norwegian Forest Cat occasionally return to the region where the animals originate, looking for good individuals that can make a valuable contribution to the continuation of the breed.

The Kuril Stumptail, for example, is a cat that

Exotic

Sphynx

was recently discovered in the Kuril Islands, a group of islands near Japan.

Travellers have also reported a lot of cats on Java with very short tails, but so far cat fanciers have shown little interest in these Javanese cats.

A number of breeds, one such being the Siamese, would normally be counted among the natural breeds, but over the last few decades selective breeding for particular characteristics and out-crosses with other breeds have removed them so far from their original form that in the area where they originate it is impossible to find a cat that meets the current standard for the breed. Breeds like this can consequently no longer be described as natural breeds.

Preceding pages: Kuril Stumptail

Persian Longhair

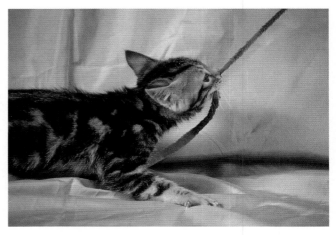

This Bengal kitten has a very determined character

Cornish Rex

Creations

Many cat breeds have been deliberately created by cat fanciers. The British Shorthair, the Bengal, the Burmese, the Persian and the Exotic are all examples of this. In developing these breeds, the breeders had a definite purpose in view.

The Persian, for example, had to be a cat with a luxuriant long coat, a stocky build, the flattest possible face and large, round eyes. Breeders consistently selected their breeding animals for these characteristics, and slowly but surely the goal was approached. Using Persians, lovers of the Exotic have created a short-haired breed of cat that looks very similar to the Persian but has a shorter coat which is not so time-consuming to look after.

The Bengal is another breed that was deliberately created. Using domestic and wild

cats, its breeders were aiming for an animal that looked as much like a wild cat as possible, but had the character of a domestic cat. The possibilities open to breeders in combining different properties of pedigree cats are effectively unlimited.

Human influence

The third group is made up of the breeds that are based on a mutant or a number of mutants

Persian Longhair

Scottish Fold

with a striking appearance. As we have seen, all cats derive from mutants, but those mutants which for one reason or another were not adequately equipped to sustain life for themselves could not survive, and consequently did not reproduce. Since people have become interested in keeping, caring for and breeding cats, however, a mutant like this can count on attracting the attention of cat fanciers who like something different. Some breeds have descended from a single mutant or a number of mutants with an unusual physical characteristic. Perhaps these animals might have managed to survive without human intervention, but we will never know.

The Scottish Fold, the various types of Rex cat, the Sphynx and the Munchkin are all examples of breeds that have descended from a single mutant or a group of mutants.

Young blue British Shorthair

Devon Rex

CHAPTER 8

Short-haired breeds

The first domestic cats were short-haired. Over time, a great many different breeds have evolved from these ancestors. A short-haired coat can be fine and virtually without an undercoat, as in the case of the Siamese, but is can also be much thicker in texture and denser, as in the British Shorthair.

In this chapter we look at a number of popular and fascinating short-haired breeds.

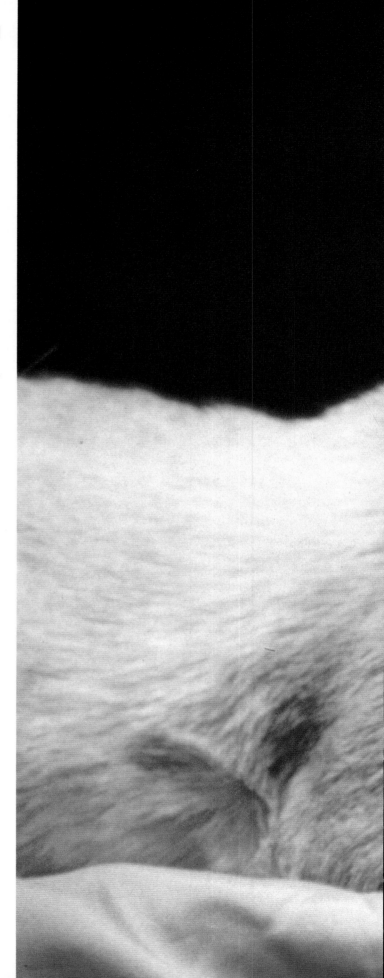

Tabby Point Siamese

Siamese

The Siamese was one of the first exotic cats to arrive in Europe. There can be very few people nowadays who would not recognize this breed. With their triangular heads, bright blue, speaking eyes and distinctive coat coloration, they are nothing if not striking.

Siamese are svelte, slender cats, who some-

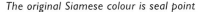

The original Siamese colour is seal point

These cinnamon and chocolate tortie point Siamese females get on very well together

The Foreign White is a variant on the Siamese. Unlike most other white cats, these cats are seldom deaf

times appear to be rather delicate, but do not be misled by this. They have well-developed muscles and can leap prodigiously. And it is not only their appearance that is distinctive; these cats have a highly individual character. Siamese cats do not hide their feelings, and are undoubtedly the most vocal cats there are. Siamese are very affectionate, and because they are also intelligent and quick-witted they can be taught a great deal.

Most Siamese are quite happy to go out for a walk on a lead, and they can also be taught to retrieve crumpled pieces of paper or soft balls. Because of this, they are sometimes described as the dogs of the cat world. Siamese do not like solitude. If you are out a lot, you would do better not to get a Siamese – or perhaps to get two so that they provide company for each other. All Siamese have a light-coloured body,

The actual colour is only seen on the head, legs and tail. The original colour is a very dark brown, known as Seal Point, but nowadays Siamese are bred in a wide range of colours.

Oriental Shorthair

Oriental Shorthairs are the same build as the Siamese and have the same sort of coat. However, there are two major differences between the breeds: the Oriental Shorthair does not have points like a Siamese, but has a self-coloured coat like other cats, and the eyes are a clear, deep green, not blue.

The character of the Oriental Shorthair is very similar to that of the Siamese. They are highly sociable, get on well with one another and with children and dogs. The coat is easy to care for. Generally speaking, it is only necessary to stroke the cat frequently, brush the coat once a week with a soft pig's bristle brush and then comb it through with a fairly fine comb. If you then smooth the fur down gently with a damp chamois leather, the coat will develop a really lovely sheen.

Oriental Shorthairs are bred in a tremendous range of colours and coat patterns, but the blue (known in Britain as the Foreign Blue) and the brown (Havana) are probably the most popular.

Abyssinian

The Abyssinian is one of the oldest known breeds. According to enthusiasts, this cat is the direct descendant of the cats that were worshipped in Ancient Egypt.

It is impossible to say with any certainty whether or not this is in fact the case but the Abyssinian, like the Siamese, is one of the first breeds to have been bred and shown by the cat fancy.

The first reported Abyssinian, a female called Zula, was brought back from Ethiopia –then known as Abyssinia– in 1871 by Field Marshal Sir Robert Napier. The Abyssinian's original coat colours are brown (also known as ruddy or usual) and sorrel – a colour known as

Oriental Shorthair

Blue Oriental Shorthair kitten

Oriental Shorthair

gradually gaining in popularity. Irrespective of their coat colour, all Abyssinians should have a coat pattern known as 'ticked tabby'. This pattern most closely resembles that of a wild rabbit.

All Abyssinians also have 'boots', darker shading at the back of the legs. People who like a cat with a traditional appearance will be attracted to this breed. Abyssinians are playful and enterprising, and they are very intelligent. They become very strongly attached to members of the family and are adept at reading their moods. They are also remarkably inquisitive – very little escapes an Abyssinian's notice.

An Abyssinian has a very definite character; he is not particularly vocal, but he has his own elegant way of letting you know exactly what it

Right: a magnificent Abyssinian with a silver undercoat

A young Abyssinian

cinnamon in other breeds and tending towards red. Many other colours have been developed over the years, including blue, chocolate and lilac.

The silver Abyssinian, another variant, is

Two young brown Abyssinians

A full-grown Abyssinian tom

is he wants you to do. This breed needs its space, both literally and figuratively, and although they will make themselves perfectly at home in a smaller house, they cannot bear to have their freedom curtailed too severely.

Russian Blue

Russian Blues are cats with a quiet, genteel nature and a slender build. Contrary to what you would expect from the name, there are also black and white forms of the breed. These aristocrats originally come from Russia and the first imports into Western Europe date from around the turn of the century. At that time, they were known as 'Archangel Blues', after the Russian port from which they were first brought to the west. There are also long-haired Russian Blues, known as Nebelung, but they are rare. Whether long or short-haired, Russian Blues need the minimum of grooming.

Russian Blue kitten

Russian Blue

Blue Burmese

Members of this attractive breed will be gentle and affectionate companions for members of the family, but they are likely to be wary of strangers.

Burmese

The Burmese is a breed of average size, of a physical type which falls between the orientals and the western short-haired breeds. One of the striking features of these cats is the subtle, pastel colour shading that seems to have been painted on to the cat with soft brush strokes. The deep sheen to the coat is another breed characteristic that shows up particularly well in the darker colours.

When Burmese lovers are asked why it is they like this breed so much, however, while the appearance will be a factor, it will certainly not be the decisive one. What attracts so many people all over the world to these cats is their friendly, extrovert and intelligent nature. The Burmese is active and playful, but can be quiet, and they are highly valued as affectionate and amusing companions. They are extremely sociable and get on very well with other cats and with dogs. They make wonderful playmates for children. The forebear of all Burmese cats was a queen called Wong Mau, who was herself not a Burmese at all, but a Tonkinese. She was brought back to the United States from Rangoon in 1930 by Joseph Thompson. These cats are bred in a wide range of colours, including brown, chocolate, blue, lilac and

Following pages: Burmese are excellent mothers

The brown Burmese has a short coat with a deep sheen

A chocolate Burmese

This British Shorthair shows the highly desirable well-developed jowls

cinnamon. The undercoat is very fine, which means that this cat requires very little grooming.

You will be able to keep the coat in superb condition simply by stroking the cat frequently and brushing the coat every so often with a soft pig's bristle brush.

British Shorthair

For years, the British Shorthair has been one of the most common and popular cat breeds in Europe. They are medium-sized to large cats, with a heavy, sturdy bone structure, a large round head and a cobby build.

Adult males of this breed are considerably larger than females and have large tomcat jowls. Almost all British Shorthairs have large, round, deep orange eyes. This striking eye colour contrasts really well with a blue coat colour, and this is perhaps one reason why the British Blue has been so popular for so long. The British Blue is sometimes mistaken for a Chartreux, but only the French blue-coated

cats are entitled to this name. British Shorthairs are bred in many different colours and coat patterns. They are found not only in all sorts of self colours, such as white, black, lilac and cream, but also in various tabby markings and with a silver undercoat, when they are known as the Chinchilla and the Shaded Silver. Outcrossing to Colour Pointed Persians recently produced Colour Pointed British Short-

A Black Silver Tabby British Shorthair, one of the most popular colours

hairs. The springy coat of the British Shorthair is beautifully soft to the touch and stands out slightly from the body. The coat is relatively easy to care for. A weekly brushing is usually enough.

As kittens, the breed can be very playful and mischievous, but as they mature they grow into good-natured, equable, placid creatures. The breed was developed in Britain around the turn of the century by crossing ordinary domestic cats and Persian Longhairs.

For many years, these cats were known outside Britain as the European Shorthair, but since the early nineteen-eighties the breed has officially been known as the British Shorthair all over the world.

Female British Shorthair

The blue British Shorthair is sometimes confused with the Chartreux

One of the latest and particularly attractive British Shorthair variants, the colour point

Sokoke

This short-haired breed with its wild appearance comes from the vast and mysterious Sokoke Forest in Kenya.

Scientists have been surprised by the existence of colonies of half-wild cats in the forest, particularly since they all had the same coat markings and colours – even the characters of the animals they found were virtually identical. Uniformity of this kind rules out any possibility that this could be a group of abandoned domestic cats; it has to be a pure breed that has lived in the forest for some considerable time. Some people believe that the cats arrived in the Sokoke Forest with western merchants hundreds of years ago and that they have remained concealed there for centuries. Others suspect that it is a breed of wild cat which has lived in the forest for much longer than that, This could explain why the local tribespeople, who refer to the domestic cat as 'Paka', have a different word in their vocabulary for the Sokoke – they call it 'Khadzonzo' (white shoulders). Sokokes prefer to hunt in trees. They show little interest in birds or birds' nests, instead devoting their energies to catching insects. At the end of the nineteen-seventies a number of Sokokes were taken to Denmark, where breeders started to develop the breed. At present the breed is still relatively rare. In order to avoid in-breeding, the few breeders working with these cats frequently go back to the Sokoke Forest in the hope of finding one or more pure-bred Sokokes to take home with them.

The Exotic's face should be a straight vertical line when viewed from the side

Exotic

In a relatively short space of time the Exotic, with its flat face, its lovable, placid nature and its easy to care for coat, has captured the hearts

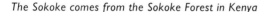

The Sokoke comes from the Sokoke Forest in Kenya

Sokoke

This young female has a good conformation and the shape of the head also meets the breed standard for the Exotic

Exotics are placid, friendly pets

of innumerable cat-lovers. There are many people who fall for the Persian's beautiful round eyes and almost human face, but are unwilling or unable to devote the considerable time and energy needed to care for that long-haired coat.

To these people, this American breed of cat makes the ideal pet. The breed was developed through crosses between American Shorthairs, Burmese and Persians. Today, outcrosses with Persians are still permitted. This means that a litter of Exotics can contain both short-haired and long-haired individuals – the latter are registered as Persian Longhairs. The breed standard for Persians and Exotics is identical, with the exception of the coat, which must be short and soft in the Exotic.

In order to prevent the Exotic from developing too long a coat, breeders occasionally mate their Exotics with American or British Short-hairs. Exotics are bred in all the coat colours accepted for the Persian.

Egyptian Mau

The Egyptian Mau is regarded as one of the oldest cat breeds in the world. Like the Abyssinian, this cat is said to have been honoured by the Ancient Egyptians. A well-known breeder of the Mau was the Russian Princess Troubetskoy, who lived in the United States and achieved widespread fame in cat

A smoke Egyptian Mau

An Egyptian Mau with beautiful tabby markings. This colour is known as bronze

Chartreux

breeding circles under the cattery name Fatima. The Egyptian Mau has a lively, active temperament. Even older cats still love to play and romp.

Although very affectionate to the family they live with, Maus are wary of strangers. They have soft voices and are not very vociferous. These cats are therefore well suited to life as flat-dwellers, provided that their owners bear in mind the amount of exercise they most definitely need.

They are bred in three colours: silver, bronze and smoke. A Mau with a smoke coat (also known as black smoke), looks like a black cat at first sight, but closer examination reveals vague tabby markings on the body. The Egyptian Mau does not require a great deal in the way of grooming.

Chartreux

There are few breeds surrounded by so many conflicting tales and legends as the Chartreux. In all probability this is an old breed of French origin.

This beautiful blue cat looks very like the blue British Shorthair. The differences in appearance are found in the size of the ears and nose, and the shape of the head. The British Shorthair has a round head, while the head of

the Chartreux is slightly triangular. The Chartreux also has a longer nose without a clear nose break, and the ears are both larger and set higher on the head.

Bengals with a light-coloured undercoat are called Snow Bengals

The eyes are often yellow rather than orange. Chartreux have a luxuriant, glossy coat, soft to the touch, with a slightly woolly undercoat. The coat colour is always blue.

These cats are friendly and placid, and make ideal pets. They are rarely found outside France and Belgium.

Bengal

The Bengal is a breed developed in the United States by crossing the domestic cat with an Asiatic leopard cat, *Felix bengalensis*. The aim was to create a breed that resembled a wild cat as closely as possible, but had an accommodating and friendly nature.

The breed is still being developed, which means that cats with a high proportion of wild blood are used for crosses now and then. Bengals are spirited, active, playful cats which get on well

> **Tip**
> The loose hairs are not always easy to remove from the coat of a short-haired cat. A rubber brush is the solution.
> Its use is not limited to brushing the cat itself; it is also extremely efficient at getting cat hair off your clothes and furnishings.

with other cats, and with dogs too. They are not the sort of cat that will spend the whole evening purring on your lap. And that is not what the Bengal enthusiasts are looking for in their cats. They are fascinated by the beautiful coat markings and the lively, unusual temperament. Bengals can have either a classic tabby pattern or a pattern of more or less extended rosettes, and the ground colour of the coat may be anything from light cream to sandy or reddish brown.

Bengal kittens with classic tabby coats

CHAPTER 9

Long-haired and semi-long-haired breeds

There is in fact only one truly long-haired breed of cats: the Persian Longhair. All other breeds with long hair are actually semi-longhairs. The Persian Longhair is also the only cat whose coat requires a great deal of care and grooming. The coat of any of the semi-longhair breeds can be kept in good condition with the minimum of effort. The most popular breeds are discussed in this chapter.

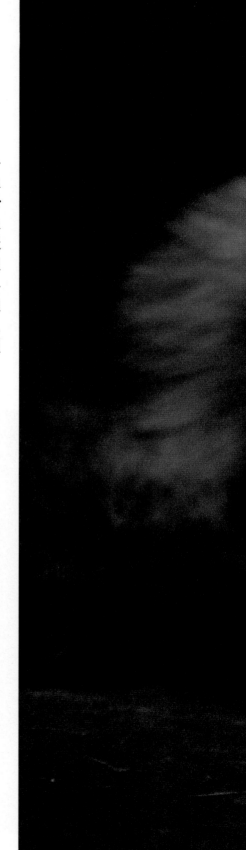

Turkish Angora, black tortoiseshell

Persian

The Persian Longhair is almost certainly the world's most popular pedigree cat breed. It is believed that the ancestors of the Persian Longhair were the semi-longhaired white cats brought back from the east on merchant vessels from the eighteenth century onwards. These cats, now known as Turkish Angoras, were very popular for many years, but around 1900 British breeders started to selectively breed them for a long, thick coat and a stockier build, and crossed them with the much cobbier British Shorthair.

Gradually they created the Persian Longhair of the type we know today. This breed is unlike any other in its coat and its conformation. The breed has a long-haired coat that lies around the body like a veil, and a luxuriant ruff. The almost flat face and the large, round eyes with which the Persian gazes wonderingly on the world are equally striking features.

Persians were originally bred primarily for a blue coat, but black and white subsequently became popular. Nowadays the Persian, like the British Shorthair and the Exotic, is one of the breeds that are bred in every conceivable colour.

Most Persians have deep orange eyes, although green eyes are permitted with some coat colours. Green really shows to best advantage in the Chinchilla Persian, which is virtually white with dark tipping to the hair creating a sort of mist over the coat. Chinchillas have black-ringed eyes and a brick red, black-

Right: Cream Persian Longhair

Persian Longhair

Black Persian Longhair

Persian Longhair kitten, colour point

rimmed nose, giving them a very elegant and sophisticated look.

White Persians may have orange eyes, but blue-eyed and odd-eyed (one blue and one orange eye) forms are also accepted.

The Persian needs thorough daily grooming to

White Persian Longhair

keep its magnificent long-haired coat looking good because the coat is quite soft and very prone to tangle. The cat's large eyes also need special care.

Anyone who is put off by the considerable amount of brushing and combing involved in looking after a cat like this will be pleased to know that there is also a short-haired form – the Exotic.

Turkish Angora

Turkish Angoras originally came from Turkey. In all likelihood, these cats were introduced into Europe as early as the seventeenth century by Italian merchants, and the Vikings had taken them to Scandinavia well before this. Prior to this time, Europeans had only ever seen the stockily-built short-haired cats that kept the vermin down on their farms.

It is therefore not surprising that these elegant, white cats with their longer coats were regarded as a very special and valuable possession. Only the wealthier Europeans could afford one of these cats. It is known, for instance, that they were kept at the French Court. Later on, these cats were imported in large numbers from their country of origin.

The Turks became worried that the breed characteristics would be lost and put a number of cats into zoos, where they are still being bred today. These are all white cats, because the Turks insist that white is the only pure-bred form and that they should have one blue and one amber eye.

Nevertheless, coloured kittens are –and always have been– born to white parents. Since crossing white cats increases the risk of deafness in the offspring, the umbrella cat associations decided that the coloured kittens should be officially recognized. Now Turkish Angoras can be found in all sorts of attractive colours.

Turkish Angoras are friendly, active, very affectionate and intelligent cats who need quite a lot of fuss and attention to keep them happy.

Female Turkish Angora, harlequin

The semi-long coat feels silky soft and requires very little care to keep it in splendid condition.

Norwegian Forest Cat

The Norwegian Forest Cat is an attractive animal with a very natural appearance and a double-layered, weatherproof, semi-long coat. It is generally accepted that the Norwegian Forest Cat descends from Turkish Angoras brought back from Turkey by the marauding Vikings when they returned to their homeland. These elegant cats are thought to have mated with the larger, short-haired local cats, gradually resulting in the animal we know today.

They are large cats with a magnificent long-haired tail and a water-repellent outer coat. Norwegian Forest Cats have occurred in the vast Norwegian forests for centuries, but they

Blue Tabby Turkish Angora male

Until recently, white was the only recognized colour for the Turkish Angora

have also been widely kept as farm cats for generations because they are superb mousers. Norway is a country rich in myth and legend, and many of the stories centre on these splendid cats.

It was not until the nineteen-thirties, however, that the breed attracted the notice of serious breeders. Now, the Norwegian Forest Cat is a familiar sight at cat shows all over the world and a much-loved family pet in many households. The coat is wonderfully thick and resilient to the touch and can be kept in good condition with the minimum of grooming because these cats rarely suffer from tangles in their fur.

This is not really surprising since they have had to look after themselves for centuries and a

Left: cream Norwegian Forest Cat

Black Tabby Norwegian Forest Cat, female

An exceptionally attractive male Black Tabby Norwegian Forest Cat

Following pages: Maine Coon, cream with white

coat that tangled easily would have jeopardized their chances of survival. The Norwegian Forest Cat may have any of the coat colours or patterns found in an ordinary farm cat. Norwegian Forest Cats are lovable, affectionate, lively cats with a sociable, tolerant nature.

Maine Coon

The Maine Coon owes the first part of its name to the state of Maine, where the breed was originally found. 'Coon' is short for raccoon. The breed was given this name because it was said that these cats, with their flowing, ringed tails, were the result of crosses between cats

and raccoons. In fact, the Maine Coon is very like the Norwegian Forest Cat and some people believe that it is a direct descendant of these cats, which they suggest were brought to North America by the Vikings.

Although this would seem quite plausible, historians are still unable to agree as to whether the Vikings ever did reach America. The Maine Coon is a friendly, equable cat with a semi-long coat. It gets on extremely well with other cats, and usually has no problems with dogs. It is good with children.

The Maine Coon is the largest domestic breed of cat, and this is reflected above all in the size and weight of the adult males.

A fully-grown tom can weigh over ten kilos (22 pounds), although it may take three years or more for him to reach his ultimate size. The Maine Coon's coat may be any of the normal

This Maine Coon has the highly desirable lynx tufts on the ears

Maine Coon female, blue tortie with white

colours and patterns found in farm cats. The texture of the Maine Coon's coat is such that it does not tangle, making it very easy to care for.

Turkish Van

The Turkish Van is a semi-longhaired cat with highly distinctive markings. The coat is chalk white, with one or two coloured patches above the eyes and a coloured tail. The most common colour is auburn, although black and tortoiseshell do occur.

Turkish Vans were discovered relatively recently by a British writer and her friend when travelling in Turkey and Armenia. The cats were living in an isolated area around Lake Van. It was not just their distinctive coloration and semi-long coat that were so striking, but

The penetrating gaze of the Turkish Van

their behaviour, which was very unlike that of other cats. They hunted not just for mice and insects, but for fish too, and they were not at all concerned about getting wet in the process.

The first Vans were introduced into Europe by the two Englishwomen, and other cats were then brought from their native region by people who had become interested in the breed. Turkish Vans are highly individual creatures who become very attached to the members of the family.

The breed usually has amber eyes, although blue-eyed and odd-eyed forms occur. The Turkish Angora and the Turkish Van come from the same country and both have a semi-long coat, but they do not come from the same region.

This means that they are two completely distinct breeds, which differ from each other in both character and conformation.

Female Turkish Van

Birman, seal point

Birman

There is a charming legend about the Birman, or Sacred Cat of Burma. It is the tale of a sapphire-eyed goddess who lived in a temple in Burma and brought people who had died back to earth in the shape of a white cat.

The golden statue of the goddess was looked after by priests. Many long-haired white cats lived in and around the temple and were cared for and protected with great reverence. One day the temple was attacked by bandits and the High Priest was found dying at the feet of the statue. As he breathed his last, one of the temple cats leapt on to his body.

The cat turned to the statute of the goddess and, as the High Priest died, the colour of the cat's coat turned to glowing gold and his eyes turned blue. Only the paws, where they were touching the High Priest's body, remained white.

Instantly, all the other temple cats took on the same appearance and, overawed by the goddess's display of power, the bandits fled. The first Birmans in Europe were a pair sent to France.

Birmans are placid companions with a gentle nature. Their magnificent coat is easy to care for since it is not prone to tangling. Kittens of

The Birman's coat is easy to care for

Birman kittens

this breed have cream-coloured bodies and the head, legs and tails are usually darker. The paws are always white.

In a show cat the markings should be as symmetrical as possible.

Balinese and Oriental Longhairs

These two elegant breeds are long-haired varieties of the Siamese and the Oriental Shorthair.

Both breeds are friendly, lively and affectionate, with a distinctively slender build. The first Balinese appeared in the United States, where long-haired kittens were spontaneously born to two Siamese parents. The breed takes its name from Balinese dancers, because the breeders felt that the cats moved in the same lithe and

This yawning blue point Balinese displays his impressive teeth

graceful way. The Oriental Longhair, which is sometimes referred to as the Javanese, came about as a result of crossing Foreign Shorthairs and Balinese, and the breeds are consequently closely related. Both breeds have soft coats with very little undercoat, which means that they can be kept in excellent condition with the minimum of care. The Oriental Longhair is bred in a virtually unlimited range of colours; the Balinese occurs in all the colours seen in the Siamese. These cats are friendly and very vocal characters, who certainly make themselves heard. They are very fond of people,

The White Foreign Longhair with one green and one blue eye is very rare

Seal Point Balinese

and generally get on well with other cats, dogs and children. Because they are so intelligent and love attention, you can quite easily teach them tricks like retrieving a ball of paper. They will also take fairly readily to walking on a lead.

Somali

The Somali has nothing to do with the country of Somalia. It is a long-haired variant of the Abyssinian, one of the oldest known cat breeds. Like the Abyssinian, the Somali is a slender cat with an intelligent and penetrating gaze. Somalis are highly individual cats and will often attach themselves to one particular member of the family. They need space if they are to feel happy. Originally Somalis were only found in two colours –ruddy or usual, and sorrel– but nowadays they are bred in many different colours. The one thing that must

Somali

always be present, however, is the highly desirable ticking in the coat. This is a tabby marking like that found in the wild rabbit, where each individual hair has bands of lighter and darker colour. Like the other breeds with semi-long hair, Somalis have a coat that is relatively easy to look after and not prone to tangling.

Usual Somali kittens

Ragdoll

For years the Ragdoll was the subject of the most fantastic tall tales. It was said that the breed had an extremely high pain threshold and would therefore often unwittingly injure itself severely. Another story was that the breed was absolutely fearless and would go completely limp, like a ragdoll, as soon as it was picked up. Neither of these stories is true. The Ragdoll is a cat like any other. It is extremely docile, good-tempered and affectionate, which is probably why it does relax completely when it is held. Ragdolls are beautiful animals with striking coloration and blue eyes. Three different coat patterns are recognized: the Colour Point has the same markings as the Siamese, the Mitted is like the Birman, and the Bi-colour has white paws, a white belly and chest, with a characteristic blaze on the forehead in the shape of an

Siberian Forest Cat kitten

inverted V. Show judges like to see a really symmetrical blaze, which should not be too narrow.

Ragdoll, colour point

Siberian Forest Cat

The Siberian Forest Cat is a Russian semi-longhair which resembles both the Norwegian Forest Cat and the Maine Coon. Little is known about the origins of this breed, but it is thought possible that these cats descend from the Norwegian Forest Cat or are direct descendants of the Turkish Angora. The breed is still fairly rare in the West, probably because few people are aware of its existence. Siberian Forest Cats require the same sort of care as the Norwegian Forest Cat; the coat colours are also similar.

Tip
The coat of a long-haired cat will stay tangle-free for longer if you regularly rub in a special grooming powder and then brush it out again. The powder removes excess grease and dirt from the coat, which looks clean and fresh again after one of these beauty treatments.

CHAPTER 10

Unusual breeds

In this chapter we look at breeds with special characteristics that certainly make them unusual.

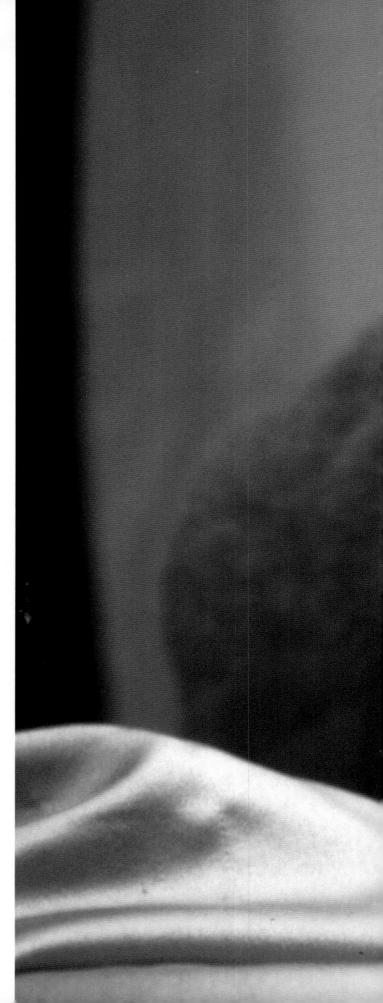

A litter of Scottish Fold kittens will include kittens with normal ears as well as kittens with the characteristic fold

Scottish Fold

The Scottish Fold is a short-haired breed with striking, folded ears. This gives the cat a very characteristic expression, which is sometimes described as owl-like. The round eyes with their surprised look reinforce this impression. The first Scottish Fold was born in the early nineteen-sixties on a farm in Perthshire, Scotland. It was a white tom, which was later named Snowball. A farm hand discovered the odd-looking cat in the straw, and thought it was sick. He took it home to his wife, who was immediately taken with Snowball. The cat later proved to be perfectly healthy and it became clear that the strange ears had been caused by a spontaneous mutation. The Scottish Fold is a friendly, good-natured cat. Although one might expect the ears to cause problems, they actually need no more care than those of other cats. Scottish Folds are never mated together, be-

Scottish Fold

cause it has been found that this produces kittens with a significant risk of skeletal abnormalities, particularly in their legs and tails. One of the parent animals must consequently have normal, upright ears. In terms of conformation, British or American Shorthairs are very like the Scottish Fold, and these breeds are therefore often used for breeding.

Long-haired Scottish Folds are called Highland Folds

Blue Scottish Fold

A litter may contain kittens with folded and normal ears. The latter are known as Scottish Straights.

Devon Rex

The Devon Rex is another breed with a highly

A Brown Tabby Devon Rex

unusual appearance. It carries its triangular head, with the large, speaking eyes, on a relatively slender neck. the Devon Rex has a curly coat. Unlike other curly-coated cats, such as the German and Cornish Rex, the guard hairs are not absent in the Devon Rex, which makes the coat feel slightly harsher. The Devon Rex is affectionate, intelligent and amusing. It is playful, active, lively and very inquisitive. These cats do not like being left alone for long, since they become very attached to 'their' people.

Cats of this striking breed are bred in all conceivable coat colours and there are also

A Devon Rex with Siamese markings is called a Si-Rex

Devon Rex

colour pointed Rexes known as Si-Rex, after the cat traditionally associated with this coloration, the Siamese.

The Devon Rex's coat requires relatively little care, but the ears do have to be cleaned regularly.

Manx

The Manx is a centuries-old breed that developed quite naturally, without human intervention, on the Isle of Man, off the coast of England in the Irish Sea. Tailless cats have occurred there for more than four hundred years.

They are highly valued as pets and as exceptionally accomplished mousers. Many scientists seem to feel that the lack of a tail

This Manx is a particularly good example of the breed

should be a handicap to the cats when hunting and climbing, but the hundreds –or possibly even thousands– of Manxes on the island who have had to fend for themselves for generations know better.

The striking breed characteristic of the Manx does not appear to hamper its movement in any way. The comparison with the lynx is obvious. Although Manx cats are highly-valued pedigree cats in many countries, on the Isle of Man they are regarded as ordinary farm cats. Tourists visiting the island can find them not just at the premises of private breeders but also out hunting in the wild.

Manxes are healthy animals with a friendly, confiding nature, which makes them ideal

The friendly look of a Manx male

Long-haired Manxes are called Cymrics

Odd-eyed Manx

Cornish Rex

The Cornish Rex is an unusual breed, with an attractive, elegant look, a wonderfully soft coat and a very friendly nature. These cats are highly intelligent and will quickly learn to walk on a lead.

The main differences between the Devon and the Cornish Rex lie in the coat and the conformation. The coat of the Devon Rex has coarse guard hairs which are absent in the Cornish Rex.

The Cornish Rex also has a different head shape. A Cornish Rex should have ripples in its coat giving a washboard effect on the back. These cats are bred in all sorts of colours, including colour point.

The coat is easy to keep in good condition by brushing the cat every so often with a soft, real bristle brush and then smoothing the coat gently with a damp chamois leather.

A very beautiful black Cornish Rex

family pets. They are found in all the colours normally associated with farm cats. The tail length can vary, but individuals with no tail at all -Rumpies- are the most highly prized for show purposes.

There are also long-haired Manx cats, which are known as Cymrics. Since the Manx and the Cymric in fact belong to the same breed –the only difference is the coat length– they are usually crossed with one another and a litter may contain both long and short-haired kittens.

The Cymric's coat is soft and semi-long, and is easy to care for. Brushing with a soft-tipped wire pin brush or combing with a coarse comb once a week is all that is needed.

Cornish Rex

Blue Cornish Rex

Sphynx

The Sphynx is perhaps the most unusual breed of all. The cat appears to be completely hairless, but if you look closely you will see that the whole body is actually covered with very short, downy hair. The effect is to make the Sphynx's skin feel like a peach.

It is sometimes said that Sphynxes have a higher constant body temperature than other cats, but this is not true. It only appears to be the case because, in the absence of a thick coat, the skin feels so warm to the touch. People often get a Sphynx because they have allergy problems, but you should be aware that this cat can cause reactions just like any other cat if the owner is allergic to dander.

Although the Sphynx's odd appearance does not appeal to everyone, it makes a sociable, friendly and affectionate pet. It gets on very well with other cats and with dogs and children. It is active and playful, and because it

has little if any fur, it is not an attractive host to parasites like fleas. The Sphynx's skin needs a degree of care.

The animal perspires and will start to smell if it is not bathed. Sphynx breeders occasionally cross a Devon Rex or ordinary domestic cat into their Sphynx bloodlines to prevent inbreeding.

Other unusual breeds

There are many other unusual breeds. The Munchkin is one of them. This cat has extremely short legs, rather reminiscent of the Dachshund. It is an American breed, which occurs in both long and short-haired forms. Munchkins are friendly, playful cats. They can climb like any other cat, but their conformation means that they cannot jump very high. Another striking cat is the American Curl with ear tips that curl backwards, giving the cat an interesting and appealing look. There are long-haired and short-haired forms of this breed which, like the Munchkin, is bred in all coat colours. Because the long-haired cats have a very thin undercoat, they require little in the way of grooming.

The American Wirehair is the only known breed with a wiry coat. The coat feels coarser than that of the Rex cats and has a different texture.

These cats are bred primarily in the United States, where they are often crossed with American Shorthairs.

Right: Sphynx, blue-cream with white

Below: Cornish Rex

Below right: a Brown Tabby Sphynx male

Index

Photography credits

All the photographs were taken by the author with the exception of the black and white illustrations. These were taken from *The Book of the Cat, Cats and All About Them, The Siamese Cat* and *Cats for Pleasure and Profit.*